MUST-KNOW

ITALIAN

MUST-KNOW
ITALIAN

4,000 Words That Give You the Power to Communicate

Daniela Gobetti

Illustrations by Jason Fennell

New York   Chicago   San Francisco   Lisbon   London   Madrid   Mexico City
Milan   New Delhi   San Juan   Seoul   Singapore   Sydney   Toronto

Copyright © 2007 by The McGraw-Hill Companies, Inc. All rights reserved. Printed in the United States of America. Except as permitted under the United States Copyright Act of 1976, no part of this publication may be reproduced or distributed in any form or by any means, or stored in a database or retrieval system, without the prior written permission of the publisher.

2 3 4 5 6 7 8 9 10 11 12 13 14 15   FGR/FGR   0 9 8 7

ISBN-13: 978-0-07-145645-6
ISBN-10:   0-07-145645-7
Library of Congress Control Number: 2006926023

Interior design by Blue Mammoth Design
Interior illustrations by Jason Fennell

McGraw-Hill books are available at special quantity discounts to use as premiums and sales promotions, or for use in corporate training programs. For more information, please write to the Director of Special Sales, Professional Publishing, McGraw-Hill, Two Penn Plaza, New York, NY 10121-2298. Or contact your local bookstore.

This book is printed on acid-free paper.

Contents

2 People and Relationships

3 Human Body, Health, and Medicine

4   Education

5   Shopping

6 A Place to Live

7 Occupations and the Business World

8 Leisure Time

9 Transportation, Traffic, and Tourism

10 Government, Politics, and Society

11 Earth, Nature, and the Environment

12   Measures, Time, and Dates

Introduction

I nterest in Italy and its language is growing. People are intrigued by Italian literature, operas, films, design, architecture, fashion, and cuisine. And visitors in Italy enjoy the company of hospitable and witty Italians.

Must-Know Italian is a compact traveling companion in which readers will find essential words for communicating in Italian, reading an Italian newspaper, and navigating an Italian website. Its four thousand entries are divided among twelve themes so that students can learn words in context. If you are traveling, you will be interested in trains, tickets, ticket counters, reservations, and so forth. If you cook, you will be thinking about pots and pans, salt and pepper. As we say in Italian, ***Una ciliegia tira l'altra*** (literally, *One cherry leads to another*), or in English, *One thing leads to another.*

Each of the twelve themes is subdivided into sections, where entries are listed in alphabetical order in English. If you don't find a word in one section, read up or down, and you are likely to find the one you are seeking. If you don't find a word in the subsection titled Diet in Chapter 3, for example, try the subsection titled Cooking at Home in Chapter 6.

You will find many English words used in the Italian translations. Italian has always incorporated words from other languages, but never more than today, when English has become the shared global language. Italians use **il cordless** (*cordless telephone*), even though we have an attractive Italian neologism for this, **il senzafili**.

I have given no Italian alternatives to words such as *film*, *sport*, and so on, because although they exist, they are not in common use. But in cases where both Italian and English versions are used indifferently, I have listed both, while giving precedence to the Italian version.

Must-Know Italian contains essential words, but not just elementary ones. In the subsection Personality and Faculties in Chapter 2, for example, there is a listing for *off-putting*—not a word you really need if you merely wish to make a hotel reservation or ask for directions. However, the Italian equivalent, **antipatico**, is so important and so frequently used as to make it indispensable.

This book contains over seventy Must-Know Tips. These address basic word usage and cultural habits. I have added **FF** (false friend) before an entry when an Italian word is a cognate of an English word but carries a different meaning, or when something in the English word suggests an Italian translation that would be completely erroneous.

Users of this guide are likely to have a grammar book already at hand. Therefore, I bring up a grammatical point only when it changes or adds to the meaning of a word or a cluster of words. For example, I mention that the word **ci** (*us*) also means *here*, and it is also used to build the expressions **c'è** and **ci sono** (*there is*, *there are*). However, if you find that you need to learn more about Italian pronouns and how they work, please refer to my *Practice Makes Perfect: Italian Pronouns and Prepositions*. This book, recently published by McGraw-Hill, clarifies the rules governing pronouns and provides useful exercises.

The phrases and sentences interspersed in this book have three functions:

- They illustrate points made in a Must-Know Tip.
- They show the contexts in which words can be used.
- They show the use of false friends—words that have similar origins but diverging meanings in the two languages.

The exercises at the back of the book are intended to help students to memorize words and practice using them. The exercises take into account the theme of each chapter and provide different levels of difficulty. For instance, talking about politics requires a more sophisticated and technical vocabulary than describing physical traits, so readers will probably find the exercises in Chapter 10 harder than the exercises in Chapters 1 and 2.

From the Renaissance until well into the nineteenth century, Italian was a language one needed to know if one were a poet, musician, diplomat, or scholar. Today we have other, new reasons for learning it: an appreciation for beauty even in humble objects, for a savory and balanced diet, and for a way of life that still balances work and play. A warm welcome to all new Italian speakers!

Reading Tips

- English verbs are listed without the preposition *to*. Therefore, when a verb and a noun have the same form in English, I have given the Italian translation of both: *hope* is both **sperare** and **la speranza**; *cost*, **costare** and **il costo**.
- The English article *the* has been omitted. Italian nouns are always accompanied by the definite article so that the gender of the word is clear: **il problema** (*problem*), **il cane** (*dog*), **la fame** (*hunger*). The labels (m&f), masculine & feminine, and (f&m), feminine & masculine, mean that the noun is used to refer to both males and females, or vice versa: **il giudice** (m&f) (male or female *judge*), **il chirurgo** (m&f) (male or female *surgeon*), **la persona** (f&m) (female or male *person*).
- Both the masculine and feminine articles are listed when the noun does not change, but the article does change according to the person's gender: **il pianista, la pianista** (male *pianist*; female *pianist*). When the final vowel of an article is replaced by an apostrophe because the following word begins with another vowel, the vowel of the article appears in parentheses: **l(a)'ancora** (*anchor*), **l(o)'osso** (*bone*).
- Plurals with regular endings have been omitted, such as **tetto, tetti** (*roof, roofs*); **casa, case** (*house, houses*); and **pesce, pesci** (*fish, fishes*), but irregular plurals have been listed: **il problema, i problemi** (*problem, problems*); **l'uovo, le uova** (*egg, eggs*).

- Adjectives are listed with the last letter ending in **-o** or in **-e**. The former change both in gender and number, depending on the word they qualify: **un uomo buono** (*a good man*), **una donna buona** (*a good woman*), **degli uomini buoni** (*good men*), **delle donne buone** (*good women*). Adjectives ending in **-e** change only in number: **un ragazzo interessante** (*an interesting boy*), **una ragazza interessante** (*an interesting girl*), **dei ragazzi interessanti** (*interesting boys*), **delle ragazze interessanti** (*interesting girls*).
- The article appears in square brackets when the word is used with or without the article, as in the case of an adjective which has also become a noun: **[il] ricco** (*the rich person, the wealthy*); or in the case of a noun used as a qualifier: **[la] vedova** → *È rimasta vedova* (*She's now a widow*); or when a noun is often preceded by a possessive: **[il] padre** → **mio, suo,** (etc.) **padre** (*my, his/her,* [etc.] *father*).
- Square brackets are placed around words that may be omitted without leaving any doubt as to the meaning of the expression: **la [santa] messa** (*mass*).
- Square brackets are also used for prepositions that usually follow a verb: **occuparsi [di]** (*deal* [*with*]).
- A semicolon separates two Italian words that translate the same English word. A semicolon also separates a verb from a noun. A backslash separates synonyms or grammatical alternatives.

MUST-KNOW
ITALIAN

1

Communicating with Others

Introductions, Greetings, and Farewells

Personal Information

address	**indirizzare; l(o)'indirizzo**
To whom did you address your letter?	*A chi hai indirizzato la lettera?*
be born	**nascere**
Elena was born on May 15, 1956.	*Elena è nata il 15 maggio 1956.*
How old are you?	*Quanti anni hai?*
I'm twenty-two years old.	*Ho ventidue anni.*
birth	**la nascita**
Do you know her place and date of birth?	*Sai quali sono il suo luogo e data di nascita?*
birthday	**il compleanno**
His birthday is July 15.	*Il suo compleanno è il 15 luglio./ Compie gli anni il 15 luglio.*
be called	**chiamarsi**
What's your name?	*Come ti chiami?*
My name is Giulia.	*Mi chiamo Giulia.*
divorced	**divorziato**
given name	**il nome proprio**
husband's name	**il nome del marito**
last name	**il cognome**
live	**vivere; abitare**
They live in Italy.	*Vivono in Italia.*
I live at 8 Via Sarpi.	*Abito in Via Sarpi 8.*

I dati personali

 Must-Know Tip

When women marry in Italy, they either take their husband's name, or add their husband's name to their own:

Elena Conti married Mario Lucchini and now signs her name Elena Conti Lucchini.

Elena Conti ha sposato Mario Lucchini e adesso si firma Elena Conti Lucchini.

maiden name	**il nome da sposare**
married	**sposato**
She's married to my brother.	*È sposata con mio fratello.*
Mr. and Mrs. Lucchini	**il signore e la signora Lucchini**
née	**nata** (only for women)
Mrs. Lucchini née Conti	**La signora Lucchini nata Conti**
nickname	**il soprannome**
occupation	**l(a)'occupazione**

 Must-Know Tip

Both **essere** and **fare** are used to convey someone's profession. **Fare** is not used, however, to indicate roles that become indistinguishable from a person's identity.

He's a factory worker.	*È un operaio./Fa l'operario.*
She's a princess.	*È una principessa.*

single	[il, la] **single; celibe** (unmarried man); **nubile** (unmarried woman)

 Must-Know Tip

Foreign words were once considered all masculine and indeclinable in Italian, but that rule is now disregarded. English words have continued to seep into Italian as you will see in the following examples.

The number of single people is growing.	*Il numero dei single è in aumento.*
He directed many films.	*Ha diretto molti films.*

widow	[la] **vedova**
widower	[il] **vedovo**

Greetings and Introductions I saluti e le presentazioni

business card	**il biglietto da visita**
doctor	**[il] dottore, [la] dottoressa**

Must-Know Tip

Dottore, Dottoressa are used not only to address physicians, but with any person who has received a **laurea** (college degree).

Dr. Monti, could you read my report on acid rain?	***Dottoressa Monti, ha potuto leggere la mia relazione sulla pioggia acida?***

farewell	**addio**
gentleman, Sir, Mr. Smith	**il signore/Signore/Signor Smith**
get in touch with	**mettersi in contatto con**
good-bye	**arrivederci** (informal)/ **arrivederla** (formal)
greet	**salutare**
How are you?	***Come stai?/Come sta?***
hello	**ciao**

Must-Know Tip

Use **ciao** *only* with people with whom you are on informal (**tu**) terms. Otherwise use the more formal **buon giorno, buona sera,** etc.

Hello, Carla, shall we walk to school together?	***Ciao, Carla, andiamo a scuola insieme?***
Hello, Mr. Brown, did you have a good trip?	***Buon giorno, Signor Brown, ha fatto buon viaggio?***

introduce	**presentare**
introduction	**la presentazione**
Pleased to meet you.	***Molto lieto./Lieto di fare la tua/sua conoscenza.***

Pleased to have met you.	*Lieto di aver fatto la tua/sua conoscenza.*
lady, Madam, Mrs. Polito	**la signora/Signora/Signora Polito**
young lady, Ms., Miss Bianchi	**la signorina/Signorina/Signorina Bianchi**
welcome	**dare il benvenuto; il benvenuto**
Welcome to my home!	*Benvenuti in casa mia!*
Welcome to Milan!	*Benvenuti a Milano!*

Manners

L(a)'educazione

accompany	**accompagnare**
I'll walk home with you.	*Ti accompagno a casa.*
answer/response	**rispondere; la risposta**
apologies	**le scuse**
apologize	**scusarsi**
ask for	**domandare [a]; chiedere [a]**
behave [well/badly]	**comportarsi [bene/male]**
Is her son behaving well in school?	*Suo figlio si comporta bene a scuola?*
behavior	**il comportamento**
be someone's turn	**toccare a qualcuno**
It's her turn.	*Tocca a lei.*
be sorry	**dispiacere**
I'm sorry.	*Mi dispiace.*
blunder	**la gaffe**
bother	**disturbare, disturbarsi; il disturbo; dare fastidio; il fastidio**
Don't bother coming to the airport. I'll take a cab.	*Non disturbarti a venire all'aeroporto. Mi prendo un taxi.*
brought up well/badly	**educato bene/male**
excuse	**scusarsi; chiedere scusa; la scusa; [chiedere] permesso**
Excuse me, may I borrow your pen?	*Mi scusi, mi impresta la penna?*
Excuse me, may I come in?	*Permesso, posso entrare?*

favor	**favorire; il favore; il piacere**
Can you do me a favor?	*Puoi farmi un favore/piacere?*
good/bad manners	**le buone/cattive maniere**
have good/bad manners	**essere beneducato/maleducato**
You have no manners!	*Lei è proprio un maleducato!*
Didn't they teach you good manners?	*Non ti hanno insegnato le buone maniere?*
impolite	**scortese; maleducato**
kind	**gentile**
It's kind of you.	*È gentile da parte tua/sua.*
kindness	**la gentilezza**
line	**la coda**
Don't cut in line!	*Non passare davanti agli altri in coda!*
mind/matter	**importare**
Never mind.	*Non importa.*
misunderstand	**capire male/fraintendere**
misunderstanding	**l(o)'equivoco**
not at all	**non c'è di che/di nulla**
please	**per favore**
Can you pass the milk, please?	*Mi passi il latte, per favore?*
politeness	**la cortesia**
question	**la domanda; la questione**
At the lecture she asked many questions.	*Ha fatto molte domande alla conferenza.*
We have to solve that question.	*Dobbiamo risolvere quella questione.*
shut up	**stare zitto; zittire [qualcuno]**
Shut up!	*Sta' zitto!*
sure	**sicuro; certo**
thank	**ringraziare; il ringraziamento** (used more often in the plural; see example below)
With my sincerest thanks, . . .	*Con i miei più sentiti ringraziamenti,...* (formal)

Many thanks!	*Grazie mille!*
Thank you.	*Grazie.*
You're welcome.	*Prego.*

Talking on the Telephone | ## Parlare al telefono

answer	**rispondere [al telefono]; la risposta**
answering machine	**la segreteria telefonica**
beep/ring	**suonare; il segnale acustico**
Please leave a message after the beep.	***Siete pregati di lasciare un messaggio dopo il segnale acustico.***
call	**chiamare; la chiamata; telefonare [a]**
call again later	**richiamare**

 Must-Know Tip

The prefix **ri-** corresponds to the English *re-*, or to the verb followed by *again*: **ridire**; **ricontare**; **rileggere**; **riscrivere** (*to say again; to recount; to reread; to rewrite*). Many verbs, however, begin with **ri/re,** but do not indicate repeating an action: **ricordare; rifiutare; rimproverare** (*to remember; to refuse; to scold*).

cell[ular] phone	**il cellulare/il telefonino**
cordless	**il senzafili; il cordless**

 Must-Know Tip

Italian adjectives can be used as nouns by adding the article. The same applies to English words that have become common in Italian: *single, cordless*, and so on.

[be] cut off	**cadere**
We were cut off.	***È caduta la linea.***
daily planner/notebook	**l(a)'agenda**
desk	**la scrivania**

dial	comporre il numero; fare il numero
Didn't I dial the right number?	*Non ho fatto il numero giusto?*

Must-Know Tip

The verb **fare** (*to do/to make*) is used to replace more technical verbs. **Lavorare a maglia** (*to knit*) becomes **fare la maglia**; **comporre un numero telefonico** (*to dial a telephone number*) becomes **fare un numero di telefono**; **cucinare** (*to cook*) becomes **far da mangiare**.

extension	[l(o)'] interno
fax machine	il fax
hang up	riattaccare
Hello!	*Pronto!*
Hello, who's speaking?	*Pronto, chi parla?*
hold	restare in linea; attendere
Can you hold, please?	*Resti (Resta) in linea, per favore.*
message	il messaggio
operator	l(o)'operatore, l(a)'operatrice
pager	il pager
phone card	la scheda telefonica
recharge	ricaricare; la ricarica
ring someone up	dare uno squillo a qualcuno
speak [to]	parlare [a/con]
Can I speak to Sara?	*Posso parlare con Sara?*
This is she.	*Sono io.*
Who is it?	*Chi parla?*
It's Enrico.	*Sono Enrico.*
spell	dire lettera per lettera; compitare
switchboard	il centralino
switchboard operator	il, la centralinista; i centralinisti, le centraliniste
telephone line	la linea telefonica
The line is busy.	*La linea è occupata.*

telephone number	il numero di telefono/telefonico
toll-free number	il numero verde
voice mail	la casella vocale/il voice mail
yellow pages	le pagine gialle

Writing a Letter

9/2/2005; September 2, 2005

Scrivere una lettera

2-9-2005; 2/9/2005; 2 settembre 2005

 Must-Know Tip

Dates follow this pattern: day of the month, month, year; **2/9/2005** or **2-9-2005** can only mean: **2 settembre 2005**. Italian uses cardinal numbers, except for the first day of the month, which should be: **1mo (primo) settembre 2005**. Otherwise, **15 agosto 2004** or **15-8-2004** (August 15, 2004). Names of months are not capitalized (*see* Chapter 12). In letter writing, the date is preceded by the name of the place where the writing occurs: **Roma, 2/9/2005**.

accent	[l(o)'] accento
apostrophe	[l(o)'] apostrofo
colon	[i] due punti (pl. only)
comma	[la] virgola
Dear Mario/Maria/Sir/Madam	Caro Mario/Cara Maria (informal)/ Gentile (or Gentilissimo) Signore/Signora (formal)

 Must-Know Tip

The name of the person addressed is followed by a comma; the following line and every line that begins a new paragraph are usually indented.

| dash/hyphen | [la] lineetta; [il] trattino |
| drop a line | mandare due righe |

ellipses	**[i] puntini [di sospensione]**
exclamation mark	**[il] punto esclamativo**
Greetings/Best greetings	**Saluti/Cordiali saluti** (informal and relatively formal)
Love,	**Con amore,/Con affetto,**
parentheses	**[la, le] parentesi**
You can put that sentence in parentheses.	***Puoi mettere quella frase in parentesi.***
period	**[il] punto; il periodo**
phrase	**la frase; l(a)'espressione**
question mark	**[il] punto interrogativo**
quotation marks	**[le] virgolette**
Regards/Best regards	**Cordialmente** (informal and relatively formal)
Respects	**Ossequi** (very formal)
semicolon	**[il] punto e virgola**
sentence	**la frase**
sign	**firmare; firmarsi**
signature	**la firma**
Sincerely	**Distinti/Rispettosi saluti** (formal)
underline	**sottolineare**
With affection	**Con affetto**
Yours	**Tuo/Suo**

Congratulations, Wishes, and Invitations
Le congratulazioni, gli auguri e gli inviti

accept	**accettare**
anniversary	**l(o)'anniversario**
Happy anniversary!	***Buon anniversario!***
announce	**annunciare**
announcement	**l(o)'annuncio**
appointment	**l(o)'appuntamento**
arrange	**fissare; stabilire**
Did we arrange a time for our meeting?	***Abbiamo fissato/stabilito l'ora della riunione?***

bring; take	**portare; prendere**
Do you want to take flowers or chocolates to our hostess?	*Vuoi prendere dei fiori o dei cioccolatini per la padrona di casa?*
Can you bring me a cup of tea?	*Puoi portarmi una tazza di tè?*
condolences	**le condoglianze**
My most heartfelt condolences.	*Le mie più sincere condoglianze.*
congratulations	**i complimenti; le congratulazioni**
console	**consolare**
gift; present	**il regalo**
give	**regalare**
gladly	**volentieri**
My parents gladly accepted their in-laws' invitation.	*I miei genitori hanno accettato volentieri l'invito dei loro consuoceri.*
inauguration	**l(a)'inaugurazione**
invite	**invitare**
invitation card	**il biglietto d'invito**
New Year's Eve dinner	**il cenone di Capodanno**
occasion	**l(a)'occasione**
offer	**offrire/l(a)'offerta**
I made him an offer he couldn't refuse.	*Gli ho fatto un'offerta che non poteva rifiutare.*
party	**la festa/il party**
punctual	**puntuale**
ready	**pronto**
receive	**ricevere**
reception	**il ricevimento; il rinfresco**
refuse	**rifiutare**
return	**ricambiare**
token	**il segno**
Accept this gold watch as a token of our appreciation.	*La preghiamo di accettare questo orologio d'oro come segno del nostro apprezzamento.*
toast	**brindare; il brindisi**
Cheers!	*Salute!/Cin cin!*

wish	desiderare; il desiderio; augurare; l(o)'augurio (often used in the plural: gli auguri)
Happy birthday!	*Buon compleanno!*
Happy New Year!	*Buon anno!*
Merry Christmas!	*Buon Natale!*
My best wishes for a speedy recovery.	*I miei migliori auguri di una pronta guarigione.*

Mail

La posta

air/ground mail	[la] posta aerea/via terra
box	la scatola
care of	presso
courier	[il] corriere
envelope	la busta
fee	la tariffa
fragile	fragile
gift-wrapped	il pacco regalo
mail; ship	spedire
mail box	la buca [delle lettere]
mail carrier	il, la portalettere; i, le portalettere
next-day delivery	[la] consegna il giorno successivo
package	impacchettare/fare il pacco; il pacco
postcard	la cartolina
post office	l'ufficio postale
post office box	la casella postale
print	scrivere a stampatello
priority mail	la posta prioritaria
recipient	il destinatario
send	mandare
sender	il mittente
stamp	il francobollo; la marca da bollo; il timbro
telegram	il telegramma

tracking	il monitoraggio
urgent	urgente
via/through	tramite
wrap	impacchettare
zip code	C.A.P. (il Codice di Avviamento Postale)

Must-Know Tip

In Italy the zip code is placed before the city's name. Italy is divided into regions and provinces. Each province has a **capoluogo di provincia** (*provincial capital*). When the address indicates a city that is not the capital of the province, a two-letter acronym for that city is added in parentheses.

Gent.le Sig.ra Anna Grassi

Via San Sepolcro 5

20146 Busto Arsizio (MI)

Italian and Foreign Cities — Città italiane ed estere

Beijing	Pechino
Berlin	Berlino
Capetown	Città del Capo
Florence	Firenze (FI)
Geneva	Ginevra
Genoa	Genova (GE)
Jerusalem	Gerusalemme
Lisbon	Lisbona
London	Londra
Milan	Milano (MI)
Moscow	Mosca
Naples	Napoli (NA)
Paris	Parigi
Prague	Praga
Rome	Roma (RM)

Stockholm	**Stoccolma**
Turin	**Torino (TO)**
Venice	**Venezia (VE)**
Warsaw	**Varsavia**

 Must-Know Tip

Italian and English use the same spelling for many names of cities: Oslo, Sydney, Bordeaux, Rotterdam, Budapest. Increasingly, Italians are using names of cities in their original language.

Parts of Speech

Articles

Gli articoli

the	**il, lo (l'), la (l'); i, gli, le (l')**
the boy and the girl	*il ragazzo e la ragazza*
the boys and the girls	*i ragazzi e le ragazze*
the egg and the eggs	*l(o)'uovo e le uova*
the ostrich and the ostriches	*lo struzzo e gli struzzi*
a, an	**un, uno, una, (un')**
a boy and a girl	*un ragazzo e una ragazza*
an egg	*un uovo*
a horse and an ostrich	*un cavallo e uno struzzo*
a soul	*un(a)'anima*

Subject Pronouns

I pronomi soggetto

subject	**il soggetto**
subjective	**soggettivo**
I	**io**
you (sing., informal)	**tu**
he	**lui**

In Italian you use the second-person singular (**tu**) to address people informally, and the third-person feminine singular (**Lei**) to address them formally.

Do you want to go skiing with us, Marco?	***Vuoi venire a sciare con noi, Marco?***
Do you want to go skiing with us, Dr. Savi?	***Vuole venire a sciare con noi, Dottor Savi?***

she	**lei**
it	**esso, essa**
you (sing., formal)	**Lei**
we	**noi**
you	**voi**
you (pl., familiar and semiformal)	**voi**
Gentlemen, you're kindly requested not to smoke.	***Signori, siete pregati di non fumare.***
they	**essi, loro**
you (pl. formal)	**Loro**

Direct Object Pronouns

I pronomi complemento oggetto

object	**l(o)'oggetto**
objective	**oggettivo**

	weak	strong
me	**mi**	**me**
you	**ti**	**te**
him	**lo**	**lui**
her	**la**	**lei**
you (sing., formal)	**La**	**Lei**
it	**lo/la**	**—**
us	**ci**	**noi**
you (pl.)	**vi**	**voi**

	weak	strong
them	li, le	loro
you (pl., formal)	Li, Le	Loro
them (objects)	li, le	—

Indirect Object Pronouns
I pronomi complemento indiretto

	weak	strong
to/for me	mi	a/per me
to/for you	ti	a/per te
to/for him	gli	a/per lui
to/for her	le	a/per lei
to/for you (sing., formal)	Le	a/per Lei
to/for us	ci	a/per noi
to/for you	vi	a/per voi
to/for them	gli	a/per loro
to/for you (pl., formal)	gli	a/per Loro

Reflexive Pronouns
I pronomi riflessivi

myself	mi
yourself	ti
himself	si
herself	si
itself	si
oneself	si
yourself (sing., formal)	si
ourselves	ci

yourselves	**vi**
themselves	**si**
yourselves (pl., formal)	**si**

Must-Know Tip

The particle **si** is also used to convey an impersonal, indefinite subject that may or may not include the speaker.

Are we going to the movies tonight?   ***Si va al cinema stasera?***

People are talking a lot about the hurricane.   ***Si parla molto dell'uragano.***

Possessive Adjectives and Pronouns
Gli aggettivi e i pronomi possessivi

my/mine	**il mio, la mia; i miei, le mie**
your/yours	**il tuo, la tua; i tuoi, le tue**
his	**il suo, la sua; i suoi, le sue**
hers	**il suo, la sua; i suoi, le sue**
its	**il suo, la sua; i suoi, le sue**
one's own	**il proprio, la propria; i propri, le proprie**
your/yours (sing., formal)	**il Suo, la Sua; i Suoi, le Sue**
our/ours	**il nostro, la nostra; i nostri, le nostre**
your/yours	**il vostro, la vostra; i vostri, le vostre**
their/theirs	**il loro, la loro; i loro, le loro**
your/yours (pl., formal)	**il Loro, la Loro; i Loro, le Loro**

Demonstrative Determiners
Gli aggettivi e i pronomi dimostrativi

this, this one	**questo, questa**
these, these ones	**questi, queste**
this (one), these (ones) over here	**questo qui/qua, questi qui/qua**
that, that one	**quello, quella**
those, those ones	**quelli, quelle**

that (one), those (ones) over there	**quello là, quelli là**
that (one), those (ones) over here	**quello lì, quelli lì**

 Must-Know Tip

Italian can use **questo**, **questa**, **quello**, and **quella** followed by an adjective to refer to someone or something already mentioned, as English does with *this one* and *that one*.

Instead of the blue umbrella, I took the red one.	***Invece dell'ombrello blu, ho preso quello rosso.***

Indefinite Pronouns / I pronomi indefiniti

a few	**alcuni; dei, delle, ecc.; qualche** (sing. only)
a little	**un po' di; poco**
Do you have any sugar? I have a little.	*Hai dello zucchero? Ne ho un po'.*
There isn't much sugar left.	*È rimasto poco zucchero.*
anyone/anybody	**chiunque** (sing. only)
each	**ciascuno/ognuno**
each other; one another	**l'un; l'altro**
everyone	**ciascuno/ognuno/tutti**
everything; entire/whole	**tutto**
few	**pochi**
much, many	**molto, molta; molti, molte**
no one/nobody	**nessuno**
nothing	**niente/nulla**
one	**uno**
other	**altro; l'altro**
Do you want more wine?	*Vuoi dell'altro vino?*
some/any/a few	**alcuni/qualcuno** (sing. only)
someone/somebody/anyone/ anybody	**qualcuno**
something/anything	**qualcosa**

Prepositions

at; to	**a**
between; among	**fra/tra**
for; through	**per**
from; by	**da**
in; at; into; to	**in**
of; about	**di**

> **Must-Know Tip**
>
> **Del**, **dello**, **della**, and so on, are also used as indefinite articles, meaning *some* and *any*.
>
> | | |
> |---|---|
> | Do you want some apples? | *Vuoi delle mele?* |
> | I don't want any apples. | *Non voglio delle mele.* |

on; over	**su**
with	**con**

Comparatives and Superlatives

I comparativi e i superlativi

as . . . as/so . . . so	**così... come**
as much/many as	**tanto, tanta... quanto, quanta;** **tanti, tante... quanti, quante**
least	**il meno**
less . . . than	**meno... di/che/di quanto, di come,** **di quello che**
less; fewer	**meno; di meno**
There is less milk than bread.	*C'è meno latte che pane.*
There are fewer cherries than oranges.	*Ci sono meno ciliege che arance.*
more . . . than	**più... di/che/di quanto, di come, di** **quello che**
She likes movies more than books.	*Le piacciono i film più dei libri.*
There are more movies than books.	*Ci sono più film che libri.*
more	**più; di più**

I'd like to see her more.	**Mi farebbe piacere vederla di più.**
more and more; larger and larger	**sempre di più; sempre più grande**
most	**il più, i più; la maggior parte**
so . . . that	**così... da/che/di quanto**

Coordinating Conjunctions — Congiunzioni coordinative

also	**anche**
and	**e, ed**
but	**ma**
either . . . or	**o... o**
however	**tuttavia**
instead [of]	**invece [di]**
neither . . . nor	**né... né**
or	**o; oppure**
otherwise	**altrimenti**
therefore	**dunque; perciò**
thus	**quindi**

Interrogative Words and Pronouns — Parole e pronomi interrogativi

How?	**Come?**
How much? How many?	**Quanto? Quanta? Quanti? Quante?**
What?	**Cosa? Che cosa?**
When?	**Quando?**
Where?	**Dove?**
What? Which?	**Quale? Quali?**
Who? Whom?	**Chi?**
Whose?	**Di chi?**
Why?	**Perché?**

Other Subordinating Conjunctions — Altre congiunzioni subordinative

after	**dopo; dopo che**
although	**sebbene**
as/so long as	**finché/fino a quando**

because	perché
before	prima di; prima che
even if	anche se
if; whether	se
that	che

 Must-Know Tip

That and **che** can also be relative pronouns, functioning as subject and direct object.

| *The man who walked out just now is my brother-in-law.* | **L'uomo che è appena uscito è mio cognato.** |
| *The movie that we saw last night was OK.* | **Il film che abbiamo visto ieri sera era OK.** |

| until | finché... non; fino a quando... non |
| while; whereas | mentre |

Miscellanea	**Varie**
Here she is!	*Eccola!*
thing	la cosa
stay	stare; rimanere; restare

 Must-Know Tip

The verb *stare* is used in the phrases:

| *How are you?* | **Come stai? Come sta? Come state?** |

And to form the present progressive:

| *I'm reading a book.* | **Sto leggendo un libro.** |

2

People and Relationships

Physical Description

Body

attractive/nice-looking

body language

cellulite

handsome/good-looking

Her husband is really handsome.

naked

pretty

sexy

shape

Vittorio is in great shape.

FF *Roberto performed really well at his job interview.*

short

slender

small

FF *They have a young child.*

stout

tall

Il corpo

attraente (said of women)

il linguaggio del corpo

la cellulite

prestante (said of men); **di bell(o)'aspetto**

Suo marito è veramente una persona di bell'aspetto.

nudo

carino (said of women and children)

sexy

la figura; la forma

Vittorio è in gran forma.

Robertó ha fatto una gran bella figura al colloquio di lavoro.

piccolo; di bassa statura

slanciato

piccolo

Hanno un bambino piccolo.

robusto

alto; di alta statura

Face

beautiful

dark

cheek

cheekbones

chin

ear

expression

eye

eyelashes

Il viso

bello

scuro

la guancia

gli zigomi

il mento

l(o)'orecchio, le orecchie

l(a)'espressione

l(o)'occhio

le ciglia

freckles	le lentiggini
light	chiaro
look like/resemble	assomigliare [a]
mouth	la bocca
nose	il naso
pale	pallido
round	rotondo
skin	la pelle
Do you have normal, dry, or oily skin, Ma'am?	*Ha la pelle normale, secca o grassa, Signora?*
ugly	brutto
wrinkle	la ruga

Hair / I capelli

bald	calvo; pelato
bangs	la frangia/la frangetta
beard	la barba
blonde	[il] biondo; [la] bionda
She's been a platinum blonde ever since the early sixties.	*È dagli anni sessanta che lei è una bionda platinata.*
braids	le trecce
brunette	castano; [la] brunetta
curls	i riccioli
dandruff	la forfora
eyebrows	le sopracciglia
goatee	il pizzo
hair	i capelli; il pelo
moustache	i baffi
pigtails	i codini
ponytail	la coda [di cavallo]
sideburns	le basette
straight	liscio
wig	la parrucca

Personality and Faculties

Personality	La personalità
aggressive	**aggressivo**
ambitious; driven	**ambizioso**
Massimo is so ambitious!	*Massimo è troppo ambizioso!*
attitude	**l(o)'atteggiamento**
His [negative] attitude is complicating things.	*Il suo atteggiamento negativo complica le cose.*
autonomous	**autonomo**
bad	**[il] cattivo**
be	**essere**
boast	**vantare; vantarsi**
calm/quiet	**calmo**
In an emergency, stay calm.	*In caso di emergenza, sta calmo.*
She's very quiet.	*È molto calma.*
character	**il carattere**
He's good-natured.	*È di buon carattere.*
charming	**affascinante**
confident	**sicuro di sé**
cunning	**furbo; la furbizia**
curious	**curioso**
defect/fault	**il difetto**
doubt	**dubitare; il dubbio**
flexible	**flessibile**

 Must-Know Tip

Buono and **cattivo**, like the English *good* and *bad*, can refer to features of people and things, animals, flavors, the weather, and so on. **Bravo** is used to indicate moral, intellectual, or artistic accomplishment.

You've really been a good kid.	***Sei stato proprio un bravo bambino.***
Be quiet, Mom has a lot to do.	***Sta bravo, che la mamma ha tanto da fare.***
Are you good in math?	***Sei brava in matematica?***

generous	**generoso**
good	**[il] buono; il bene; bravo**
great/remarkable	**notevole; grande** (said of an exceptional human being)
have	**avere; possedere**
humble	**umile**
individual	**l(o)'individuo** (m&f)
individualist	**[l(o, a)'] individualista**
laid-back	**indolente**
lazy	**pigro**
lively	**vivace**
nastiness	**la cattiveria**
nasty	**cattivo; malvagio**
naughty	**malizioso; birichino** (said of children)
nice	**simpatico**
modest	**modesto**
off-putting	**antipatico; scostante**
optimist	**[l(o, a)'] ottimista**
ordinary	**normale; ordinario** (derogatory)
overbearing	**[il] prepotente**
That jerk took my parking place!	*Quel prepotente mi ha rubato il parcheggio!*
patient	**paziente**
person	**la persona** (f&m)
pessimist	**[il, la] pessimista**
picky	**difficile**
pleasant	**piacevole; gradevole**
The weather today is pleasant.	*Il tempo oggi è piacevole.*
profound	**profondo**
proud	**orgoglioso**
respected	**stimato**
His father is well-respected as a surgeon.	*Suo padre è un chirurgo molto stimato.*
sense of humor	**il senso dell'umorismo**

Elena has a great sense of humor.	*Elena ha un ottimo senso dell'umorismo.*
serious	**serio**
shy	**timido**
silly	**[lo] sciocco**
stiff	**rigido**
stingy	**[l(o)'] avaro**
strict	**severo**
strong	**forte**
superficial	**superficiale**
sweet	**dolce**

 Must-Know Tip

In Italian you can convey a superlative by repeating an adjective or an adverb: **dolce dolce** (*very sweet*), **grande grande** (*very large*), **piccolo piccolo** (*very small*), **vicino vicino** (*very close*), **lontano lontano** (*far away*), **bene bene** (*very good*), **sì sì** (*yes, indeed*), **no no** (*absolutely not*), **così così** (*so, so*). Long words, however, are not repeated: **importante importante** (*very important*) sounds clumsy.

temperament	**il temperamento**
tough	**[il] duro**
trivial	**insignificante; frivolo**
type (of person), guy	**il tipo; la tipa**
She's a cheerful type.	*È un tipo allegro.*
vain	**vanitoso**
weak	**debole**
weakness	**la debolezza; il debole [per]**
weird/strange	**strano**
wise	**[il] saggio**

Emotions and Passions — Le emozioni e le passioni

admire	**ammirare**
afraid	**spaventato**

Must-Know Tip

Aver[e] paura translates *to be afraid* (literally: *to have fear*). In Italian we say **avere fame**, **ragione**, **sete**, **sonno**, and **torto** (*to be hungry*, *right*, *thirsty*, *sleepy*, and *wrong*).

anger/wrath	**l(a)'ira; la rabbia**
annoy/irritate	**irritare; fare fastidio**
anxious	**ansioso**
appreciate	**comprendere; rendersi conto**
I appreciate your predicament.	*Mi rendo conto che sei in un momento difficile.*
bear; support	**sopportare**
be concerned/worried	**preoccuparsi**
be homesick	**avere nostalgia**
She left Australia after a year because she was homesick.	*È ripartita dall'Australia dopo un anno perché aveva troppa nostalgia di casa.*
be preoccupied	**pensare ad altro**
FF Don't worry. We'll find a solution.	*Non preoccuparti, troveremo una soluzione.*
bore	**annoiare; la noia**
boring	**noioso**
compassion	**la compassione**
cheerful	**allegro**
close [to]	**vicino [a]**
confuse	**confondere; confondersi**
desperate	**disperato**
disappoint	**deludere**
embarrassed	**imbarazzato**
emotional	**emotivo/emozionale**
envious	**invidioso**
fear	**temere; la paura**
feel	**sentire; sentirsi; provare simpatia [per]**

My daughter does not feel well.	*Mia figlia non si sente bene.*
She lost both her parents when she was very young. I really feel for her.	*Ha perso entrambi i genitori da piccola. Provo tanta simpatia per lei.*
feeling	**la sensazione; l(a)'emozione; il feeling**
get angry	**arrabbiarsi**
happy	**felice**

 Must-Know Tip

The prefix **in-** (**im-** before **-b** and **-p**) corresponds to the prefixes *in-/im-* and *un-* in English.

She's been very unhappy since her divorce. **Da quando ha divorziato è molto infelice.**

have it in for	**avercela con**
hope	**sperare; la speranza**
intriguing	**intrigante**
You've had a really intriguing idea.	*Hai avuto un'idea proprio intrigante.*
FF Be careful what you tell him; he's a meddler.	*Stai attenta a quello che gli dici, perché è un intrigante.*
jealous	**geloso**
melancholy	**la malinconia; malinconico**
mood	**l(o)'umore**
My father is always in a good mood.	*Mio padre è sempre di buon umore.*
move; be touched (with emotion)	**muovere; commuovere; commuoversi**
I'm moved.	*Sono commosso.*
nervous	**nervoso**
panic	**il panico**
passion	**la passione**
perhaps/maybe	**forse**
resign oneself to	**rassegnarsi a**
restless	**agitato; inquieto**

sad	**triste**
sorrow	**il dolore**
support	**sostenere; il sostegno; il supporto**
unbearable	**insopportabile**
unburden oneself	**sfogarsi**

Mental and Psychological Faculties and Actions

Le facoltà mentali e psicologiche e le azioni

absentminded	**distratto**
act	**agire; recitare**
action	**l(a)'azione**
active	**attivo**
anyway	**in ogni caso/comunque**
appear/seem	**apparire/sembrare**
It seems that the government wants to raise taxes.	*Sembra che il governo voglia aumentare le tasse.*
as usual	**come al solito**
aware	**cosciente; consapevole**
be able to; can; may	**potere**

 Must-Know Tip

Dovere, **potere**, **sapere** (meaning *to know*), and **volere** can be followed by another verb in the infinitive. When the meaning is *to succeed*, it is better to use **riuscire a** than **potere**.

Finally he succeeded in talking to her.	*Finalmente è riuscito a parlare con lei.*

become	**diventare**
become aware	**accorgersi; rendersi conto**
She's aware that her marriage is in trouble.	*Si rende conto che il suo matrimonio è in crisi.*
Did you realize that the dog has stopped eating?	*Ti sei accorta che il cane ha smesso di mangiare?*
be necessary	**essere necessario; bisogna**

Must-Know Tip

Bisogna also translates as *must*. It is impersonal and used only in a few tenses and modes in the third-person singular.

We must pay taxes by May 30. **Bisogna pagare le tasse entro il 30 maggio.**

be used to [+ *gerund*]	**essere abituato a; avere l(a)'abitudine di** [+ *infinitive*]
Victoria is used to cooking for ten people.	*Vittoria è abituata a cucinare per dieci.*
by all means	**senz(a)'altro**
by no means	**assolutamente no**
capable	**capace**
She's very capable.	*È molto capace.*
She's capable of just about everything.	*È una capace di tutto.*
conscience; consciousness	**la coscienza**
consequence	**la conseguenza**
convince	**convincere**
dare	**osare**
deal [with]	**occuparsi [di]**
decide	**decidere**
depend [on]	**dipendere [da]**
It doesn't depend on me whether he gets that job.	*Non dipende da me che lui ottenga quel lavoro.*
disappear	**scomparire**
distinguish	**distinguere**
do; make	**fare**
dream	**sognare; il sogno**
easygoing/relaxed	**disinvolto**
fail	**fallire**
fault	**la colpa**
It's all my fault if he lost his job.	*È tutta colpa mia se ha perso il lavoro.*

Must-Know Tip

The verb **fare** can take the idiomatic form **farcela** (**fare** + the adverb of place **ci/ce** + **la**, used as a generic pronoun referring to the action being done). It means: a) *to manage, to (barely) be able to*; and b) *to succeed, to make it.*

Do you need help with that suitcase? No, I can make it.	**Hai bisogno di aiuto con quella valigia? No, ce la faccio [da solo].**
I did it! I biked 100 kilometers in a day!	**Ce l'ho fatta! Ho fatto cento chilometri in bici in un giorno!**

forget	**dimenticare; dimenticarsi [di]**
get	**ottenere; diventare**
Her sister always gets what she wants.	*Sua sorella ottiene sempre quello che vuole.*
His parents got rich.	*I suoi genitori sono diventati ricchi.*
give in	**cedere**
His father gave in and let him take the Ferrari.	*Suo padre ha ceduto e gli ha lasciato prendere la Ferrari.*
give up	**rinunciare [a]**
Did they give up building a house at the sea?	*Hanno rinunciato a costruire la casa al mare?*
habit	**l(a)'abitudine**
idea	**l(a)'idea**
FF Did they change their minds?	*Hanno cambiato idea?*
imagination	**l(a)'immaginazione; la fantasia**
instinct	**l(o)'istinto**
intelligence	**l(a)'intelligenza**
intention	**l(a)'intenzione**
irrational	**irrazionale**
know	**conoscere; sapere**

Must-Know Tip

We use **conoscere** to convey that we are/are not acquainted with someone. We use **sapere** to convey that we have knowledge or information about someone or something.

Do you know her parents?	***Conosci i suoi genitori?***
Do you know where she went?	***Sai dov'è andata?***

let	**lasciare**
Let him read in peace!	***Lascialo leggere in pace!***
like	**piacere; aver[e] voglia di**

Must-Know Tip

The verb **piacere** (as well as **bastare** [*to be sufficient to*], **far bene** or **far male** [*to be good* or *bad for*], **importare** [*to matter*], **mancare** [*to lack/to miss*], **succedere** [*to happen*], etc.) turns the object of the action into the subject of the sentence, and the person to whom the action happens into the indirect object.

I like ice cream.	***Mi piace il gelato.***
Ice cream is good for you.	***Il gelato ti fa bene.***

make do	**arrangiarsi; rimediare**
Did you find the screwdriver? No, but I made do with a coin.	***Hai trovato il cacciavite? No, ma mi sono arrangiata con una monetina.***
manage/cope	**cavarsela**
The test was very difficult, but I managed to pass it.	***L'esame era molto difficile, ma sono riuscito a cavarmela.***
memory	**la memoria; il ricordo**
mind	**importare; dispiacere; la mente**
I'd like to smoke a cigarette if you don't mind.	***Vorrei fumare una sigaretta se non ti dispiace.***

Keep in mind that she cannot walk very fast.	*Ricordati/Tieni a mente che lei non può camminare velocemente.*
motive	**il motivo**
FF I love that tune.	*Mi piace molto quel motivo.*
must/have to/shall	**dovere**

need	**aver bisogno [di]; il bisogno**
passive	**passivo**
pretend	**far finta di; pretendere**
Just for fun, she pretends to be her twin sister.	*Per divertimento, fa finta di essere la sua gemella.*
FF He claims to be entitled to damage compensations.	*Pretende il risarcimento dei danni.*
rational	**razionale**
react	**reagire**
reality	**la realtà**
realize	**realizzare**
Pietro realized his dream to go to Tahiti.	*Pietro ha realizzato il suo sogno di andare a Tahiti.*
really	**veramente; davvero; proprio**
They're really rich.	*Sono veramente ricchi.*
Is it really true that the senator's father was a war criminal?	*È proprio vero che il padre del senatore era un criminale di guerra?*
Her boss was arrested. Really?!	*Il suo principale è stato arrestato. Davvero?!*
reason	**ragionare; la ragione**

reflect [on]	**riflettere [su]**
Did you reflect on my advice?	***Hai riflettuto sul mio consiglio?***
The clear water of the pond reflected the surrounding mountains.	***Le chiare acque del laghetto riflettevano le montagne circostanti.***
remember	**ricordare; ricordarsi [di]**
remind someone of something	**ricordare qualcosa a qualcuno**
Remind me to buy some butter.	***Ricordami di comprare il burro.***
smart	**intelligente; astuto**
stupid	**stupido**
subconscious	**[il] subconscio/[il] subcosciente**
suppose	**supporre**
surprise	**soprendere; la sorpresa**
think [of/about]	**pensare [a qualcuno/qualcosa]**
I thought I would do him a favor.	***Pensavo di fargli un favore.***
I think so. (I don't think so.)	***Penso di sì. (Penso di no.)***
thoughts	**i pensieri**
You're in my thoughts.	***Sei nei miei pensieri.***
try [to]	**provare [a]; cercare [di]; tentare [di]**

Must-Know Tip

The prefix **dis-/s-** conveys the meanings of the English *un-* , added before a verb or an adjective: **fare** (*do*) → **disfare/sfare** (*undo*); **coprire** (*cover*) → **scoprire** (*uncover*); **dire** (*say*) → **disdire** (*cancel*); and so on. Several verbs, however, convey meanings separate from their etymological origins: **discutere** (*discuss*); **disintegrare** → (*disintegrate*); **distruggere** (*destroy*); **disperdere** (*disperse*); and **scoprire** (*discover*), which is a separate translation from **scoprire** previously in this paragraph.

understand	**capire**
undo	**disfare**
use	**usare**

want	**volere; avere voglia di**
will	**volere; la volontà**

Family Relations

Family

La famiglia

affection	**l(o)'affetto**
agree	**essere d'accordo; andare d'accordo**
You two agree on just about everything.	***Voi due andate d'accordo praticamente su tutto.***
argue	**litigare**
aunt	**[la] zia**
baby	**il neonato; il bebè**
best man	**il testimone** (at a wedding)
boyfriend	**il [mio, tuo, ecc.] ragazzo**
bride	**la sposa**
brother	**[il] fratello**

brother-in-law	**il cognato**
care [for]	**voler bene [a]; essere affezionato [a]**

She loves her children a lot.	**Vuole molto bene ai suoi figli.**
children	**i bambini** (until adolescence); **i figli**
cohabit	**convivere**
companion, partner	**il, la [mio, mia, tuo, tua, ecc.] compagno; il partner**
couple; pair	**la coppia; il paio, le paia**
They make a nice couple.	**Sono una bella coppia.**
They have been an item for a year now.	**È da un anno che fanno coppia fissa.**
He bought three pairs of gloves.	**Ha comprato tre paia di guanti.**
I have two tickets for the opera.	**Ho un paio di biglietti per l'opera.**
cousin	**[il] cugino**
cradle	**cullare; la culla**
dad	**[il] papà**
daughter	**[la] figlia**
daughter-in-law	**[la] nuora**
discuss	**discutere**
discussion	**la discussione**
divorce	**divorziare; il divorzio**
embrace	**abbracciare; abbracciarsi**
engagement	**il fidanzamento**
ex/former husband, fiancé, etc.	**il mio ex (marito, fidanzato, ecc.); la mia ex**
familial; familiar	**familiare/famigliare**
family tree	**l(o)'albero genealogico**
father	**[il] padre**
father-in-law	**[il] suocero**
Her father-in-law gave her a fur coat when she had her first child.	**Suo suocero le ha regalato una pelliccia quando ha avuto il primo figlio.**
fiancé, fiancée	**[il] fidanzato, [la] fidanzata**
forgive	**perdonare**
get pregnant	**restare incinta**
girlfriend	**la [mia, tua, ecc.] ragazza**
grandchildren	**i nipoti**

My grandson and granddaughter have lunch with me every Thursday.	*Mio nipote e mia nipote vengono a pranzare da me ogni giovedì.*
grandparents	**i nonni**
Grandpa and grandma are coming for Christmas!	*Il nonno e la nonna vengono da noi a Natale!*
groom	**lo sposo**
heir	**l(o)'erede; l(a)'ereditiera**
honeymoon	**la luna di miele**
husband	**[il] marito**
inherit	**ereditare**
in-laws	**i suoceri**
in love	**[l(o)'] innamorato**
People in love don't listen to anyone.	*Gli innamorati non ascoltano nessuno.*
intimate	**intimo**
kid	**il ragazzino**
love	**amare; l(o)'amore**
lover	**l(o, a)'amante**
lullaby	**la ninna-nanna**
maid of honor	**la testimone** (at a wedding)
marriage	**il matrimonio**
marry	**sposarsi**
Just married!	*Oggi sposi!*
mom	**[la] mamma**
mother	**[la] madre**
Your mother doesn't want you to eat so many sweets.	*Tua madre non vuole che tu mangi tante caramelle.*
mother-in-law	**la suocera**
neglect	**trascurare**
nephew	**[il] nipote**
niece	**[la] nipote**
parents	**i genitori**

punish	**punire**
reconcile	**riconciliare**
refrain	**trattenersi**
relatives	**i parenti**
scold	**rimproverare**
separate	**separare; separarsi**
siblings	**i fratelli [e le sorelle]**
sister	**[la] sorella**
sister-in-law	**[la] cognata**
son	**[il] figlio**
son-in-law	**[il] genero**
spoil	**viziare**
spoiled	**viziato**
stepchildren	**i figliastri**

trouble	**il guaio, i guai**
trust	**fidarsi di; la fiducia**
twins	**i gemelli, le gemelle**
uncle	**[lo] zio**
wedding	**il matrimonio (la cerimonia nuziale); le nozze**

wedding ring	la fede [nuziale]
wife	[la] moglie

Friendship and Other Relationships

L(a)'amicizia e gli altri rapporti sociali

acquaintance	la conoscenza
Pleased to make your acquaintance, Madam.	*Sono lieta di fare la sua conoscenza, Signora.*
affair	la relazione [extraconiugale]
alone	solo; da solo
He prefers to be alone.	*Preferisce stare da solo.*
She feels very lonely.	*Si sente molto sola.*
I did it myself.	*L'ho fatto da sola.*
awesome	incredibile; pazzesco
This magician is awesome!	*Questo mago è incredibile!*
boss	il boss; il [mio] principale (m&f); il [mio] capo, la [mia] capa (rare)
busy	[molto] impegnato/occupato
chat	chiacchierare; la chiacchierata
colleague/coworker	il, la collega; i colleghi, le colleghe
comment	commentare; il commento
company	la compagnia
conversation	la conversazione
court	corteggiare
ease	agio
She isn't at ease with her boss's wife.	*Non è a suo agio con la moglie del suo capo.*
expect	aspettarsi
expectation	l(a)'aspettativa
extraterrestrial	[l(o, a)'] extraterrestre; gli, le extraterrestri
flirt	flirtare; il flirt
foreign	straniero
foreigner	lo straniero
frequent	frequentare; frequente
friend	l'amico

gossip	**spettegolare; il pettegolezzo** (used more often in the plural, **i pettegolezzi**)
They gossip about everyone and everything.	*Spettegolano su tutto e su tutti.*
help	**aiutare; l(o)'aiuto**
joke	**scherzare; lo scherzo**
kid sitting next to you in class	**il compagno di banco**
loneliness; solitude	**la solitudine**
meet (someone; with someone)	**incontrare (qualcuno); incontrarsi (con qualcuno)**
I met my friend at the park.	*Ho incontrato la mia amica al parco.*
Let's meet in Piazza Navona.	*Incontriamoci in Piazza Navona.*
neighbor	**il vicino [di casa]**
Our neighbor doesn't even say hello.	*Il nostro vicino di casa non saluta neppure.*
neighborhood	**il quartiere; il vicinato**
This neighborhood has many trees.	*Questo quartiere ha molti alberi.*
She's always had good relations with her neighbors.	*Ha sempre tenuto buoni rapporti di vicinato.*
offend	**offendere**
organize; arrange	**organizzare; combinare**
My brother organized the entire trip.	*Mio fratello ha combinato tutto il viaggio.*
pay a visit [to]	**andare a trovare [qualcuno]**
people	**la gente, le genti; le persone**
Did you see how many people went to the rally?	*Hai visto quanta gente è andata alla manifestazione?*
According to the opinion polls, ninety percent of the people agree with the president.	*Secondo i sondaggi, il novanta per cento della popolazione è d'accordo con il presidente.*
personable/sociable	**socievole**
personal	**[il] personale**
FF He isn't a member of the staff.	*Non è un membro del personale.*

pick [up]	passare a prendere; far su; raccogliere
Can you pick me up at eight?	*Puoi passare a prendermi alle otto?*
I don't like that bar. Someone's always trying to pick you up.	*Non mi piace quel bar. C'è sempre qualcuno che cerca di farti su.*
She picked up the toys the baby threw on the floor.	*Ha raccolto i giocattoli che il bambino ha gettato a terra.*
promise	**promettere; la promessa**
recognize	**riconoscere**
rumor	**la diceria**
FF You're making a lot of noise!	*Fate un rumore incredibile!*
solitary	**solitario**
stranger	**l'estraneo; lo sconosciuto**
unfriendly	**poco socievole**
visit	**visitare; far visita a; la visita**
wait	**aspettare; l(a)'attesa**
womanizer	**il donnaiolo**

Nations and Religion

Continents and Countries

Continenti e paesi

Africa	**[l(a)'] Africa**
America	**[l(a)'] America**
The American continent is divided into North, Central, and South America.	*Il continente americano è diviso in America del Nord, del Centro e del Sud.*
Antarctica	**[l(a)'] Antartide**
Asia	**[l(a)'] Asia**
Brazil	**[il] Brazile**
China	**[la] Cina**
country	**il paese; la campagna** (countryside)
Russia is a huge country.	*La Russia è un paese molto vasto.*
We spent last summer in the country.	*Abbiamo passato l'estate scorsa in campagna.*

Europe	[l(a)'] Europa
Great Britain	[la] Gran Bretagna
Great Britain consists of England, Scotland, Wales, and Northern Ireland.	*La Gran Bretagna è composta dall'Inghilterra, la Scozia, il Galles e l'Irlanda del Nord.*
Hungary	[l(a)'] Ungheria
Italy	[l(a)'] Italia
Japan	[il] Giappone
Jordan	[la] Giordania
Middle East	[il] Medio Oriente
New Zealand	[la] Nuova Zelanda
Norway	[la] Norvegia
Oceania	[l(o)'] Oceania
Spain	[la] Spagna
Sweden	[la] Svezia
Switzerland	[la] Svizzera
The Netherlands/Holland	i Paesi Bassi/[l(a)'] Olanda
Turkey	[la] Turchia
United States of America	gli Stati Uniti [d'America]/gli USA

Populations and Languages Popoli e lingue

accent	l(o)'accento
American	americano

 Must-Know Tip

Adjectives or nouns indicating populations and languages end mostly in **-ano, -ana, -ani,** and **-ane** (**americano, americana, americani, americane**); or in **-ese,** or **- esi** (**francese, francesi**). Names of nationalities and languages are not capitalized.

The French really love good cuisine. ***I francesi adorano la buona cucina.***

Arab; Arabic	[l(o)]'arabo
bilingual	bilingue

Chinese	[il] cinese
customs/mores	gli usi; i costumi
dialect	il dialetto
dictionary	il dizionario; il vocabolario
English	[l(o)'] inglese
French	[il] francese
Greek	[il] greco
Hebrew	[l(o)'] ebraico
interpreter	l(o, a)'interprete
mother tongue	la madre lingua/la lingua madre
Portuguese	[il] portoghese
sign language	la lingua dei segni
Spaniard; Spanish	[lo] spagnolo
speak	parlare
speech	il discorso; la parola
The president of the republic gave a fine speech.	*Il presidente della repubblica ha fatto un bel discorso.*
Speech is a characteristic of the human species.	*La parola è una caratteristica della specie umana.*
translate	tradurre
She translates Spanish into Russian.	*Traduce dallo spagnolo al russo.*
translation	la traduzione
tribe	la tribù, le tribù
Turk; Turkish	[il] turco
vocabulary	il lessico
word	la parola

Religion and Religions

La religione e le religioni

alms	l(a)'elemosina
angel	l(o)'angelo
Every evening the children say a prayer to their guardian angel.	*Ogni sera i bambini dicono una preghiera all'angelo custode.*
atheism	l(o)'ateismo
believe	credere
Many people don't believe in God.	*Sono in tanti a non credere in Dio.*

I believe you.	***Ti credo./Credo a te.***
believer	**il, la credente**
Bible	**la Bibbia**
bishop	**il vescovo**
Buddhism	**il buddismo**
cardinal	**il cardinale**
Catholicism	**il cattolicesimo**
charity	**la carità**
Christian	**[il] cristiano**
Christianity	**il cristianesimo**
church	**la chiesa; la Chiesa**
clergy	**il clero**
creation	**la creazione**
creature	**la creatura**
cross	**la croce**
curse/swear	**bestemmiare; la bestemmia**
damnation	**la dannazione**
devil	**il diavolo**
evil	**il male**
faith	**la fede**
fundamentalism	**il fondamentalismo**
God; god	**Dio; il dio, gli dei**
For Christians, God is three persons:	***Per i cristiani, Dio è tre persone: il***
Father, Son, and Holy Spirit.	***Padre, il Figlio e lo Spirito Santo.***
Heaven	**[il] Cielo**
Hinduism	**l(o)'induismo**
Islam	**l(o)'Islam**
Islamic	**islamico**
Jewish	**[l(o)'] ebreo**
Judaism	**il giudaismo/l(o)'ebraismo**
lay person	**[il] laico**
mass	**la [santa] messa**
monastery	**il monastero**
monk	**il monaco**
mosque	**la moschea**

Muslim	[il] musulmano
myth	il mito
nun	la suora
Old Testament; New Testament	il Vecchio Testamento; il Nuovo Testamento
Orthodox	ortodosso
pagan	[il] pagano
pilgrimage	il pellegrinaggio
pope	il papa
pray	pregare
prayer	la preghiera
priest	il prete; il sacerdote
Protestant	[il, la] protestante
Protestantism	il protestantesimo
religious	[il] religioso
remorse	il rimorso
resurrection	la resurezione
rite	il rito
sacraments	i sacramenti
Catholics believe in seven sacraments.	*I cattolici credono in sette sacramenti.*
saint	il santo
salvation	la salvezza
sect	la setta
sin	peccare; il peccato
soul	l(a)'anima
temple	il tempio
thy neighbor	il [tuo] prossimo
Virgin Mary	la Vergine Maria/la Madonna
worship	adorare; il culto

3

Human Body, Health, and Medicine

Body, Senses, and the Mind

Body: Structure and Main Organs

	Il corpo: struttura e organi principali
artery	l(a)'arteria
blood	il sangue
bone	l(o)'osso, le ossa (of human beings); gli ossi (of animals)
brain	il cervello
flesh	la carne
heart	il cuore
intestine	l(o)'intestino
kidney	il rene
ligament	il legamento
liver	il fegato
lung	il polmone
muscle	il muscolo
nerve	il nervo
penis	il pene
rib	la costola
skeleton	lo scheletro
skull	il cranio
spine	la spina dorsale; la colonna vertebrale
tendon	il tendine
uterus	l(o)'utero
vagina	la vagina
vein	la vena

Head and Face

	La testa e la faccia
breath/wind	il fiato
breathe	respirare
cry/sob	singhiozzare
forehead	la fronte
hiccup	il singhiozzo
laugh	ridere; la risata

They had a good laugh.	*Si sono fatti una bella risata.*
nape of the neck	**la nuca**
neck	**il collo**
smile	**sorridere; il sorriso**
spit	**sputare; lo sputo**
tear	**la lacrima**
throat	**la gola**
weep	**piangere**
whistle	**fischiare; fischiettare**

Mouth — La bocca

chew	**masticare**
kiss	**baciare; il bacio**
lips	**le labbra**
palate	**il palato**
swallow	**inghiottire**
tongue	**la lingua**
FF How many languages can she speak?	*Quante lingue parla?*
tooth	**il dente**

Arms and Hands — Le braccia e le mani

at hand	**a portata di mano**
elbow	**il gomito**
finger	**il dito, le dita**
fist	**il pugno**
handy	**comodo; pratico**
hold; keep	**tenere**
Keep the necklace; I don't wear it anymore.	*Tieni la collana, tanto io non la metto più.*
Hold on tight to the rope!	*Tieniti stretto alla corda!*
left	**[la] sinistra**
point	**indicare; il punto**
pull	**tirare**
push	**spingere; la spinta**
right	**[la] destra**

thumb	**il pollice**
wrist	**il polso**

Torso / **Il torso**

back	**la schiena**
bottom	**il sedere**
breast	**il seno**
chest; bosom	**il petto**
digest	**digerire**
hips	**i fianchi; le anche**
stomach	**lo stomaco; la pancia**
waist	**la vita**

Legs and Feet / **Le gambe e i piedi**

ankle	**la caviglia**
heel	**il tallone**
knee	**il ginocchio, le ginocchia**
Ever since she broke her knee, she cannot kneel.	*Da quando si è rotta il ginocchio non riesce più a inginocchiarsi.*
thigh	**la coscia**
toes	**le dita dei piedi**
walk	**camminare; la camminata**

Five Senses / **I cinque sensi**

aloud	**ad alta voce**
blind	**[il] cieco**
blindness	**la cecità**
color blind	**dal tonico**
deaf	**[il] sordo**
disgusting	**disgustoso**
distasteful	**di cattivo gusto**
hear	**sentire**
hearing	**l(o)'udito**
listen to	**ascoltare**
look at	**guardare**
loud	**alto** [volume]; **troppo alto**

Turn down the volume! It's too loud!	*Abbassa il volume! È troppo alto!*
mute	**[il] muto**
see	**vedere**
sensation	**la sensazione**
sensitive	**sensibile**
FF Her grandmother was a sensible woman, but not a very sensitive one.	*Sua nonna era una donna sensata, ma non molto sensibile.*
sight/vision	**la vista**
sixth sense	**il sesto senso**
smell	**sentire un odore; l'odorato**
His dog has no sense of smell, poor thing.	*Il suo cane non ha il senso dell'odorato, poveretto.*
sound	**suonare; il suono**
stink	**puzzare; la puzza**
taste	**assaggiare; il gusto**
touch	**toccare; il tatto**

Health and Hygiene

Hygiene and Makeup

L(a)'igiene e il trucco

absorbent cotton	**il cotone idrofilo**
brush one's teeth	**lavarsi i denti**
comb one's hair	**pettinarsi**

 Must-Know Tip

In Italian many reflexive verbs carry a direct object: **pettinarsi i capelli** (*to comb one's hair*); **bagnarsi i vestiti** (*to get one's clothes wet*); **asciugarsi le mani** (*to dry one's hands*); **truccarsi il viso** (*to put on one's makeup*); **tagliarsi i capelli** (*to have one's hair cut*), **soffiarsi il naso** (*to blow one's nose*), and so on.

contagious	**contagioso**
Leprosy is a horrible disease, but not highly contagious.	*La lebbra è una malattia orribile, ma non molto contagiosa.*

deodorant	**il deodorante**
disinfect	**disinfettare**
disinfectant	**il disinfettante**
epidemic	**l(a)'epidemia**
eyeliner	**l(o)'eyeliner**
facial cream	**la crema per il viso**
infection	**l(a)'infezione**
Measles and chicken pox are infectious diseases typical of childhood.	*Il morbillo e la varicella sono malattie infettive tipiche dell'infanzia.*
lipstick	**il rossetto**
makeup	**il trucco**
Don't you take your makeup off before going to bed?	*Non ti strucchi prima di andare a dormire?*
pandemic	**la pandemia**
parasite	**il parassita**
perfume	**il profumo**
prevention	**la prevenzione**
put on makeup	**truccarsi**
remove one's makeup	**struccarsi**
quarantine	**la quarantina**
sanitary napkin	**il pannolino; il pannolone**
shampoo	**lo shampoo**
shave	**radersi; farsi la barba**
spread	**diffondersi; la diffusione**
sterilize	**sterilizzare**
sweat	**sudare; il sudore**
take a bath; take a shower	**fare il bagno; fare la doccia**
tampon	**il tampone**
tissue	**il fazzoletto [di carta]; il kleenex**
vaccine	**il vaccino**
wash	**lavarsi [le mani, i capelli, ecc.]**

Diet

La dieta

be good; be bad for someone	**far bene; far male a qualcuno**
Aunt Elena did a lot of good for many people throughout her life.	*Zia Elena ha fatto del bene a tante persone durante la sua vita.*

balanced	**bilianciato**
fast food	**il fast food**
fat	**grasso**
go on a diet	**mettersi a dieta**
lose weight	**dimagrire**
low-carb	**a basso contenuto di carboidrati**
macrobiotic	**macrobiotico**
Mediterranean	**mediterraneo**
nutritional	**nutritivo/nutrizionale**
nutritious	**nutriente**
Soy isn't very tasty, but it is nutritious.	*La soia non sa di molto, ma è nutriente.*
obese	**obeso**
overweight	**sovrappeso**
put on/gain weight	**ingrassare**
regimen/diet	**il regime; la dieta**
thin	**magro**
vegetarian	**vegetariano**
He's been a vegetarian for many years, but recently he's become a vegan.	*È stato vegetariano per anni, ma di recente è diventato vegetaliano.*
weigh	**pesare; pesarsi**
How much do you weigh?	*Quanto pesi?*
weight	**il peso**
well-being/wellness	**il benessere**

Illnesses, Disabilities, and Medical Care

Illnesses and Ailments

Malattie e malesseri

ache	**far male; il mal [di]**
My tooth aches.	*Mi fa male un dente.*
I have a headache.	*Ho mal di testa.*
bacteria	**i batteri**
be in pain	**soffrire; aver[e] male[a]**
burn	**bruciare; bruciarsi; la bruciatura; l(a)'ustione**

She burned herself with hot milk.	*Si è ustionata con il latte bollente.*
chronic	**cronico**
conscious	**cosciente; consapevole**
constipation	**la stitichezza/la costipazione [da raffreddamento]**
I need a mild laxative for constipation.	*Ho bisogno di un lassativo dolce per la stitichezza.*
FF *I caught a cold because I didn't change my wet clothes.*	*Sono costipato/raffreddato perché non mi sono tolto i vestiti bagnati.*
cramp	**il crampo**
diarrhea	**la diarrea**
fatigue	**la fatica**
faint	**svenire**
feel nauseous	**avere la nausea**
feel/be under the weather	**non sentirsi bene; sentirsi poco bene**
feel/be well	**sentirsi bene**
genetic	**genetico**
heal	**rimarginarsi** (of a wound); **guarire**
hereditary	**ereditario**
hurt	**far male; farsi male**
My head hurts.	*Mi fa male la testa.*
I hurt my head.	*Mi sono fatto male alla testa.*

 Must-Know Tip

Italian uses the preposition **a** + the definite article (**al, allo, alla, alle,** etc.) to convey where pain is located:

I hurt my arm.	*Mi sono fatta male al braccio.*
I feel pain in my arm.	*Ho un dolore al braccio.*

---

ill/sick [person]	**[il] malato/[l(o')] ammalato**
get sick	**ammalarsi**
Did he get really sick?	*Si è ammalato gravemente?*
inflammation	**l(a)'infiammazione**

migraine	l(a)'emicrania
pain	il dolore
painful	doloroso
poison	avvelenare; il veleno
revive	rinvenire
scar	la cicatrice
shock	scioccare; lo shock
Two weeks after the accident, she's still in shock.	*A due settimane dell'incidente, è ancora sotto shock.*
I'm shocked.	*Sono scioccata.*
sleepwalking	il sonnambulismo
throw up	vomitare
unconscious	non cosciente; [l(o, a)'] incosciente
FF *Only a mad man drives a motorbike on the sidewalk!*	*Solo un incosciente va in moto sul marciapiede!*
virus	il virus, i virus

Colds and Gastrointestinal Ailments / Malattie del raffreddamento e gastrointestinali

acid reflux	il riflusso [gastrico]
allergy	l(a)'allergia
bronchitis	la bronchite
catch	prendere; prendersi
catch a cold	prendere/prendersi un raffreddore
cold (virus)	il raffreddore
cough	tossire; la tosse
fever	la febbre
flu	l(a)'influenza
gallstones	i calcoli alla cistifellea
hepatitis	l(a)'epatite
indigestion	l(a)'indigestione
liver disease	il mal di fegato
phlegm	il catarro
pneumonia	la polmonite
shiver	tremare

sneeze	**starnutire; lo starnuto**
snore	**russare**
take care of oneself	**riguardarsi**
You should take care of yourself.	***Dovresti riguardarti.***

Chronic and Life-Threatening Disorders

Malattie croniche e potenzialmente letali

Alzheimer's disease	**il morbo di Alzheimer**

 Must-Know Tip

Most ailments named after people are the same in Italian as in English: **il morbo di Parkinson** (Parkinson's disease), **il morbo di Alzheimer** (Alzheimer's disease), etc.

AIDS (acquired immuno-deficiency syndrome)	**l(a)'AIDS (la sindrome da immunodeficienza acquisita)**
arthritis	**l(a)'artrite**
autism	**l(o)'autismo**
cancer	**il cancro**
coma	**il coma**
concussion	**la commozione cerebrale**
diabetes	**il diabete**
disabled	**[il, la] disabile/[l(o)'] handicappato**
dizziness	**le vertigini**
Down syndrome	**la sindrome di Down**
heart attack	**l(o)'attacco di cuore; l(o)'infarto**
herpes	**l(o)'herpes**
HIV negative or positive	**sieronegativo; sieropositivo**
immune system	**il sistema immunitario**
incurable	**incurabile; inguaribile**
metastasis	**la metastasi**

multiple sclerosis	**la sclerosi multipla**
muscular dystrophy	**la distrofia muscolare**
Parkinson's disease	**il morbo di Parkinson**
stroke	**il colpo [apoplettico]; l(o)'ictus**
The stroke left her paralyzed on the left side.	*L'ictus l'ha lasciata paralizzata dal lato sinistro.*
terminal	**terminale**
tuberculosis; TB	**la tubercolosi; la TBC**

Medical Care · L'assistenza medica

acupuncture	**l(a)'agopuntura**
alternative	**alternativo**
ambulance	**l(a)'ambulanza**
anesthesia	**l(a)'anestesia**
blood pressure	**la pressione del sangue**
caretaker	**la badante** (usually female)
We hired a caretaker for my mother, who can't live alone any longer.	*Abbiamo assunto una badante per mia madre, perché non può più vivere da sola.*
checkup	**il check-up**
cholesterol	**il colesterolo**
compatible	**compatibile**
complication	**la complicazione**
cure	**guarire [qualcuno]; la cura**
diagnosis	**la diagnosi**
E.R.	**il pronto soccorso**
fracture	**la frattura**
get over	**passare [a qualcuno]**
Finally the kids have gotten over that bad sore throat!	*Finalmente ai bambini è passato quel brutto mal di gola!*
gynecologist	**il ginecologo**
health	**la salute**
healthy	**sano; in salute**
homeopathic	**omeopatico**

Must-Know Tip

Italian can use **in** + place noun to emphasize the function of a place rather than its physical location: **in ospedale** (*in/to the hospital*); **in sala operatoria** (*in/into the operating room*); **in farmacia** (*in/to the pharmacy*), **in clinica** (*in/to the clinic*).

Let's go to the clinic.   **Andiamo in clinica.**

hospital	**l(o)'ospedale**
intensive care unit/ICU	**il reparto [di] rianimazione**
invasive	**invasivo**
medical chart	**la cartella clinica**
midwife	**l(a)'ostetrica; la levatrice**
MRI	**la risonanza magnetica**
My sister suffers from claustrophobia; she'll never do an MRI.	*Mia sorella soffre di claustrofobia, non farà mai la risonanza magnetica.*
nurse	**l(o)'infermiere, l(a)'infermiera; gli infermieri, le infermiere**
operate	**operare**
organ	**l(o)'organo**
pacemaker	**il pacemaker**
patient	**il, la paziente**
pediatrician	**il, la pediatra; i pediatri, le pediatre**
physical therapist	**il, la fisioterapista; i fisioterapisti, le fisioterapiste**
physical therapy	**la fisioterapia**
physician/doctor	**il medico** (m&f) **/il dottore, la dottoressa**
I found a good doctor.	*Ho trovato un bravo medico.*
plastic surgery	**la chirugia plastica**
primary care physician	**il medico di base**
radiologist	**il radiologo**
release; discharge	**dimettere**
recover	**guarire**

rejection	il rigetto
remedy	rimediare; il rimedio
Finally they found an effective	*Finalmente hanno trovato un*
remedy against the common cold.	*rimedio efficace contro il*
	raffreddore.
[in] remission	[in] remissione
resuscitation	la rianimazione
scrubs	il camice, la mascherina e i guanti
	[chirurgici]
sonogram	l(a)'ecografia
stretcher	la barella
surgeon	il chirurgo
surgery	la chirurgia
symptom	il sintomo
test	l(o)'esame; il test
thermometer	il termometro
transfusion	la trasfusione
transplant	trapiantare; il trapianto
treat	curare
visit	visitare; la visita
ward	il reparto
X-rays	i raggi [X]; la radiografia

Psychological Conditions and Addictions

Malattie della psiche e tossicodipendenze

alcoholic	[l(o)'] alcolizzato; l(o, a)'alcolista;
	gli alcolisti, le alcoliste
alcoholism	l(o)'alcolismo
anorexia	l(a)'anoressia
anxiety	l(a)'ansia
bulimia	la bulimia
cocaine	la cocaina/la coca
depression	la depressione
detox	disintossicarsi; la disintossicazione
drug	la droga; la sostanza stupefacente;
	il medicinale

drug abuse	**la tossicodipendenza**
drunk	**[l(o)'] ubriaco; l(a)'ubriacona**
ecstasy	**l(a)'ecstasy**
joint (marijuana)	**lo spinello**
insomnia	**l(a)'insonnia**
madness/insanity	**la pazzia**
marijuana	**la marijuana**
meth [amphetamines]	**[le] met[anfetamine]**
mental health clinic	**la clinica per le malattie mentali**
neurosis	**la nevrosi**
paranoia	**la paranoia**
psychiatrist	**lo, la psichiatra; gli psichiatri, le psichiatre**
psychoanalyst	**lo, la psicanalista; gli psicanalisti, le psicanaliste**
psychologist	**lo psicologo**
schizophrenia	**la schizofrenia**
smoke	**fumare; il fumo**

 Must-Know Tip

Signs alerting people that a certain action is forbidden are always intro-duce by **Vietato** + *infinitive* or **Divieto di** + either an infinitive or a noun (*It is forbidden/prohibited to . . .*):

Do not enter.	***Vietato l'ingresso.***
No smoking.	***Vietato fumare.***
Post no bills.	***Divieto di affissione.***

teetotaler	**astemio**
withdrawal symptoms	**i sintomi da astinenza**

Medications | I medicinali

antiallergy medications	**gli antiallergici**
antibiotics	**gli antibiotici**
bandage	**bendare; la benda; fasciare, la fasciatura**

Band-Aid	il cerotto
cold and flu remedies	gli antifebbrili e gli antinfluenzali
dosage	la dose
drops	le gocce
injection	la puntura
morphine	la morfina
nicotine patch	il cerotto antifumo
pain relief medicine	l(o)'antidolorifico/l(o)'analgesico
pharmacist	il, la farmacista; i farmacisti, le farmaciste
pill	la pastiglia; la pillola (anticoncezienale)
prescription	la ricetta
FF That isn't a medical prescription, it's a recipe!	*Quella non è una ricetta medica, ma una ricetta di cucina!*
side effects	gli effetti collaterali
sleeping pill	il sonnifero

Dental Care / La cura dei denti

abscess	l(o)'ascesso
braces	l'apparecchio [funzionale]
cavity	la carie, le carie
crown	la capsula
dental cleaning	la detartrasi; la pulizia dei denti
dentist	il, la dentista; i dentisti
dentures	la dentiera
extraction	l(a)'estrazione
gums	le gengive
hygienist	l(o, a)'igienista; gli igienisti, le igieniste
wisdom teeth	i denti del giudizio

Eye Care / La cura degli occhi

astigmatic	astigmatico
contact lenses	le lenti a contatto
eye doctor	l(o, a)'oculista; gli oculisti, le oculiste

eyeglasses	gli occhiali
Have you seen my sunglasses?	*Hai visto i miei occhiali da sole?*
farsighted	presbite
nearsighted	miope
progressive lenses	le lenti multifocali
sight impaired/visually handicapped	non vedente

Life and Death

Stages of Life

Le fasi della vita

abortion	l(o)'aborto
adolescence	l'adolescenza
adolescent	[l(o, a)'] adolescente
adoption	l(a)'adozione
adult	[l(o)'] adulto
age	invecchiare; l(a)'età
In Italy and the United States, one comes of age at eighteen.	*In Italia e negli Stati Uniti si diventa maggiorenni a diciott'anni.*
alive	vivo
artificial insemination	l(a)'inseminazione artificiale
be in labor	avere le doglie
birthrate; death rate	il tasso di natalità; il tasso di mortalità
breast-feed	allattare
childbirth/delivery	il parto
childhood	l(a)'infanzia
contraception	la contraccezione
There are several methods of contraception.	*Ci sono molti metodi contraccettivi.*
elderly	[l(o, a)'] anziano; gli anziani
exist	esistere
existence	l(a)'esistenza
fetus	il feto
foster care	l(o)'affidamento
gender	il sesso; il genere

The doctor told them the gender of the baby.	*Il dottore gli ha detto il sesso del bambino.*
give birth to	**dare alla luce**
grow [up]	**crescere**
have sex	**avere rapporti sessuali**
heterosexual/straight	**[l(o, a)'] eterosessuale**
homosexual/gay	**[l(o, a)'] omosessuale/[il] gay**
impotence	**l(a)'impotenza**
lesbian	**[la] lesbica**
live	**vivere**
man	**l(o)'uomo**
Many people still use man *to mean* humankind.	*Molta gente usa ancora il termine* **l'uomo** *con il significato di* **genere umano.**
menopause	**la menopausa**
menstruation/period	**la mestruazione**
middle age	**la mezza età**
old [people]	**[il] vecchio; [i] vecchi**
old age	**la vecchiaia**
Old age starts much later now.	*La vecchiaia adesso incomincia molto più tardi.*
orgasm	**l(o)'orgasmo**
ovulation	**l(a)'ovulazione**
ovule	**l(o)'ovulo**
pregnancy	**la gravidanza**
puberty	**la pubertà**
raise	**allevare; tirare su**
reproduction	**la riproduzione**
self-preservation	**l(a)'autoconservazione**
sex	**il sesso**
sperma	**lo sperma**
sterility	**la sterilità**
transgender/transsexual	**[il, la] transessuale**
turn on	**eccitare**
virgin	**[il, la] vergine**
wean	**svezzare**

woman	la donna
young [people]	[il] giovane, [i] giovani
youth	la giovinezza; la gioventù

Death / La morte

assisted suicide	l(a)'eutanasia assistita
autopsy	l(a)'autopsia
burial	la sepoltura
bury	seppellire
cemetery	il cimitero
coffin	la bara
commit suicide	suicidarsi
He committed suicide.	*Si è suicidato.*
corpse	il cadavere; il corpo
cremation	la cremazione
dead	[il] morto
deceased/late	[il] defunto
The late Mr. Monti was always kind to everyone.	*Il defunto signor Monti è sempre stato gentile con tutti.*
die	morire
euthanasia	l(a)'eutanasia
funeral	il funerale
funeral home	l(a)'impresa di pompe funebri
grave	la fossa
immortal	[l(o)'] immortale; gli immortali
living will	il testamento biologico; la dichiarazione anticipata di volontà di trattamento
mortal	[il] mortale; i mortali
mourning	il lutto
suicide	il suicidio
tomb	la tomba

4

Education

Education and School Subjects

Primary Education

attend

attendance

attention

Pay attention to what your teacher says.

class

In my elementary school there are five third-grade classes.

compare

concentrate

concept

correct

dictate

dictation

difficult

diligent

easy

effort

elementary school

engage; interest

explain

homework

hopeless/incompetent

My brother is hopeless at math.

ignorant

intelligent

learn

learning

mistake

nursery school

I can't find a place for my daughter in nursery school.

obedient

L(a)'istruzione primaria

frequentare

la frequenza

l(a)'attenzione

Fa' attenzione a quello che dice la maestra.

la classe

Nella mia scuola ci sono cinque sezioni della classe terza elementare.

paragonare

concentrarsi

il concetto

correggere; corretto

dettare

il dettato

difficile

diligente

facile

lo sforzo

la scuola elementare/le elementari

impegnare; interessare

spiegare

i compiti a casa

negato

Mio fratello è negato per la matematica.

[l(o, a)'] ignorante

intelligente

imparare

l(o)'apprendimento

l(o)'errore

l(o)'asilo [nido]

Non riesco a trovare un posto per mia figlia all'asilo nido.

obbediente

pupil	l(o)'alunno; l(o)'allievo
reward	premiare; il premio
school year	l(a)'anno scolastico
study	studiare; lo studio
substitute teacher	il, la supplente
talent	la dote; il talento
teach	insegnare
teacher	l(o, a)'insegnante; il maestro (only in elementary school)
teaching	l(o)'insegnamento
Teaching is a profession that requires a strong personal commitment.	*L'insegnamento è una professione che richiede un grosso impegno personale.*
try hard	sforzarsi

Middle School and High School

La scuola media inferiore e superiore

high school graduate	il diplomato
lyceum	il liceo
A lyceum is a type of high school that prepares one for college.	*Il liceo è un tipo di scuola media superiore che prepara agli studi universiari.*
middle school	la scuola media/le medie
professional/vocational school	la scuola professionale/tecnica
student	lo studente, la studentessa
teacher board	il consiglio dei professori
update	aggiornare; aggiornarsi

School Subjects

Le materie scolastiche

algebra	[l(a)'] algebra
arithmetic	[l(a)'] aritmetica
art history	[la] storia dell'arte
biology	[la] biologia
chemistry	[la] chimica
civics	[l(a)'] educazione civica
drawing	[il] disegno

foreign language	[la] lingua straniera
geography	[la] geografia
geometry	[la] geometria
history	[la] storia
Latin	[il] latino

Exams, Grades, and Degrees

Gli esami, i voti e i titoli di studio

admission test	l(o)'esame di ammissione
board exam	l(o)'esame di stato
compulsory education	la scuola dell'obbligo
certification	l(a)'abilitazione
My sister has gotten her certification to teach French.	*Mia sorella ha preso l'abilitazione per insegnare il francese.*
degree	il titolo di studio
exam	l(o)'esame
fail	non prendere la sufficienza; prendere un(a)' insufficienza; fallire; non superare
She failed the test in Latin again.	*Ha preso un'altra insufficienza di latino.*
grade	dare il voto; il voto
hold back one year	bocciare
pass	passare; prendere la sufficienza
I barely passed the test in algebra class.	*Ho preso a malapena la sufficienza nel compito in classe di algebra.*
promote to the next grade	promuovere

Classroom Procedures, Materials, and Equipment

In the Classroom

In classe

anthology	l(a)'antologia
atlas	l(a)'atlante
backpack	il sacco

ballpoint pen	**la biro/la penna a sfera**
be absent/present	**essere assente/presente**
blackboard	**la lavagna**
calculator	**il calcolatore**
cheat	**copiare**
He was expelled because they discovered he was cheating.	***È stato espulso perché hanno scoperto che copiava agli esami.***
composition	**il tema**
desk	**il banco**
discipline	**disciplinare; la disciplina**
drop; withdraw [from a course]	**ritirarsi [da un corso]**
encyclopedia	**l(a)'enciclopedia**
expel	**espellere**
felt-tip pen	**il pennarello**
in-class test	**il compito in classe**
marker; highlighter	**l(o)'evidenziatore**
notebook	**il quaderno**
pencil	**la matita**
play hooky	**tagliare**
recess	**l(o)'intervallo**
report card	**la pagella**
roll call	**l(o)'appello**
rubber band	**l(o)'elastico**
summary	**il riassunto**
suspend	**sospendere**
take notes	**prendere appunti**
teamwork	**il lavoro di gruppo**
textbook	**il libro di testo**
type	**scrivere a macchina**
typewriter	**la macchina da scrivere**

Computers and Hardware

I computer e l(o)'hardware

battery	**la pila**
FF She plays the drums constantly, day and night.	***Suona la batteria a tutte le ore del giorno e della notte.***

burn a CD	**masterizzare un CD**
computer	**l(o)'elaboratore elettronico; il computer**

 Must-Know Tip

For computer and electronic terms, Italian borrows most words directly from English. Pronunciation is at times "Italianized," and the word order follows the rules of Italian grammar.

I bought a very fast, powerful, and expensive PC.	**Ho comprato un PC (pee chee) velocissimo, potentissimo e carissimo.**

crash	**avere un crash; il crash**
cursor	**il cursore**
electronics	**l(a)'elettronica**
diskette	**il dischetto**
information technology	**[l(a)'] informatica**
laptop	**il portatile; il laptop**
memory (ROM and RAM)	**la memoria (ROM e RAM)**
mouse	**il mouse**
print	**stampare; la stampa**
printer	**la stampante**
return key	**il tasto di ritorno**
scanner	**il lettore ottico di caratteri; lo scanner**
screen	**schermare; lo schermo**
support	**supportare; il supporto**

Computer Software — Il software

back	**duplicare; fare un backup**
broadband	**la banda larga**
by default	**per default**
click	**cliccare; il click**

copy	**copiare; la copia**
cybernetics	**la cibernetica; l(a)'intelligenza artificiale**
cyberspace	**il ciberspazio**
Is cyberspace, or virtual space, as infinite as physical space?	*Il ciberspazio, lo spazio virtuale, è infinito come lo spazio fisico?*
databank	**la banca dati**
delete	**eliminare/cancellare**
digit	**la cifra**
digitalize	**digitalizzare**
display	**la videata**
download	**scaricare**
enter	**inserire**
It took her three days, but she managed to enter all the raw data.	*Le ci sono voluti tre giorni, ma è riuscita a inserire tutti i dati grezzi.*
file	**archiviare; il file**
hacker	**l(o)'hacker** (m&f)
icon	**l(a)'icona**
interface	**l(a)'interfaccia**
key in	**digitare**
press	**premere**
programmer	**il programmatore, la programmatrice**
reboot	**riavviare il sistema/fare il reboot**
save	**salvare**
shut down	**spegnere; lo spegnimento**
standby	**sospendere; la sospensione; lo standby**
My computer is in standby mode.	*Il mio computer è in standby.*
transmit	**trasmettere**
upload	**caricare**
I uploaded such a big program that my computer crashed.	*Ho caricato un programma così grosso che il mio computer ha avuto un crash.*

Internet and E-Mail

@/at

My e-mail address is: cookie "at" megaset "dot" com.

attachment

chat

e-mail

e-mail message

My e-mail box is full of spam.

forward

home page

IMS (Instant Message System)

Internet

log in/off

menu

navigate

online; off-line

password

portal

search engine

send

site

user

user-friendly

The new version of PowerPoint is really user-friendly.

videogame

L(a)'Internet e la posta elettronica

[la] chiocciola

Il mio indirizzo di posta elettronica è: cookie 'chiocciola' megaset 'punto' com.

l(o)'allegato

chattare [online]

la posta elettronica/l(o/a)'e-mail

il messaggio di posta elettronica/l(o/a)'e-mail

La mia casella di posta elettronica è piena di messaggi spam.

inoltrare

l(a)'home page

SMS/l(o)'esse emme esse (Short Message System)

l(a)'Internet

fare il log in/connettersi; fare il log off/disconnettersi

il menu

navigare

in linea/on-line; off-line

la parola d'ordine; la password

il portale

il motore di ricerca

mandare/inviare

il sito

l(o, a)'utente

user friendly/facile da usare

La nuova versione di PowerPoint è davvero user friendly.

il videogioco/il videogame

Higher Education and Long-Distance Learning

Higher Education	L(a)'istruzione universitaria
admit	**ammettere [a]**
application	**la domanda [di ammissione]**
apply [to/for]	**fare domanda [a/per]**
assistant professor; researcher	**il ricercatore**
credentials	**i titoli; le credenziali**
chair	**presiedere; la cattedra**

 Must-Know Tip

In the United States, a *chair* is a teaching position funded by an endowment. In Italy a **cattedra** is any core curriculum course taught by a full professor, assigned through national competition.

She was appointed full professor of constitutional law.	***Ha vinto la cattedra di diritto costituzionale.***

chairperson	**il, la preside**
college; university	**l(a)'università**
FF She was sent to boarding school when she was just ten years old.	***L'hanno mandata in collegio quando aveva solo dieci anni.***
college degree	**la laurea**
conference	**il convegno; il congresso**
course	**il corso**
You've taken too few mandatory courses and too many electives.	***Hai preso troppo pochi corsi obbligatori e troppi corsi facoltativi.***
credits	**i crediti**
curriculum	**il curricolo; il piano di studio**
defend one's dissertation	**discutere la tesi/la dissertazione**
department	**il dipartimento**

enroll in [the] university	iscriversi all'università
faculty	la facoltà
At the meeting of the entire faculty, her motion was rejected.	*Alla riunione di tutta la facoltà, la sua mozione non è passata.*
fellowship/scholarship	la borsa di studio
graduate [from university]	laureare; laurearsi; il laureato; postlauream
lecture	la lezione; la conferenza
library	la biblioteca
FF You said we would meet at the library! I meant at the bookstore!	*Hai detto di trovarci in biblioteca! Volevo dire in libreria!*
librarian	il bibliotecario
M.A. program	il programma di Master
Ph.D. program	il dottorato di ricerca
professor	il professore (m&f); la professoressa
rector	il rettore
research	la ricerca
room and board	[il] vitto e [l(o)'] alloggio
sabbatical year	l(o)'anno sabbatico
seminar	il seminario
syllabus	il sillabo
teaching assistant	l(o, a)'assistente
tenured	confermato; di ruolo
tuition fees	le tasse universitarie
tutoring	il tutorato
with distinction	con lode; cum laude

University and Postgraduate Schools

L(a)'università e l'istruzione postuniversitaria

Agriculture	Agraria
Business School	la Scuola di Amministrazione/ Direzione Aziendale
Classics	Lettere Classiche

Computer Science	**Informatica**
Conservatory	**il Conservatorio**
Economics	**Economia**
Education/Pedagogy	**Scienze della Formazione/Pedagogia**
Foreign Languages and Literature	**Lingue e Letterature Straniere**
joint degree (with other departments or universities)	**[il] corso di laurea interfacoltà e interateneo**
Law	**Giurisprudenza**
Mathematics, Physics, and Natural Sciences	**Matematica e le Scienze Fisiche e Naturali**
Medicine and Surgery	**Medicina e Chirurgia**
[Modern] Literature and Philosophy	**Lettere [Moderne] e Filosofia**
Pharmacology	**Farmacologia**
Physical Education	**Educazione Fisica**
Political Science	**Scienze Politiche**
Polytechnic	**il Politecnico**
Polytechnic consists of the colleges of Architecture and Engineering.	*Il Politecnico è composto dalle facoltà di Architettura e Ingegneria.*
Psychology	**Psicologia**

Distance Learning

L(o)'apprendimento a distanza

assessment	**la valutazione**
basic	**di base**
best practice	**la pratica migliore**
customize	**personalizzare**
expertise	**la specializzazione**
face-to-face	**faccia a faccia**
feedback	**il feedback; la retroazione**
information	**l(a)'informazione, le informazioni**
input	**l(o)'input; i dati [da elaborare]**
instructions	**le istruzioni**

instructor	**l(o)'istruttore**
interactive	**interattivo**
know-how	**il know-how**
method	**il metodo**
modular	**modulare**
outcome; result	**il risultato**
output	**l(o)'output; i dati elaborati**
participation	**la partecipazione**
platform	**la piattaforma**
simulation	**la simulazione**
standard	**[lo] standard**
technology	**la tecnologia**
tool	**lo strumento**
trial run	**il percorso di prova**

5

Shopping

Buying and Selling, Customer Service, and Transactions

Consumer Society

La società dei consumi

afford	**permettersi**
Can you really afford to buy a Rolls Royce?	***Puoi davvero permetterti una Rolls Royce?***
article; item	**l(o)'articolo**
average	**medio**
be worth/worthy	**valere; meritare**
That painting is worth 10,000 euros.	***Quel quadro vale 10.000 euro.***
It's worth it.	***Ne vale la pena.***
Their proposal isn't even worthy of our consideration.	***La loro proposta non merita neppure di essere presa in considerazione.***
consume	**consumare**
FF That sweater is worn out.	***Quel golf è tutto consumato.***
consumer	**il consumatore, la consumatrice**
From the producer direct to the consumer!	***Dal produttore al consumatore!***
consumerism	**il consumismo**
do errands	**fare le commissioni**
go shopping	**andare a fare la spesa/le spese; andare a fare acquisti**
indispensable	**indispensabile**
lifestyle	**lo stile di vita**
luxury	**il lusso**
The market for luxury products continues to grow.	***Il mercato dei prodotti di lusso continua a crescere.***
pay	**pagare**
status symbol	**il simbolo di status/lo status symbol**
stuff	**la roba**
You should see how much stuff she has in her closet!	***Devi vedere quanta roba ha nell'armadio!***

Buying and Selling

bargain	l(o)'affare
It's a bargain!	*È un affare!*
be convenient	essere conveniente; convenire [a]
You travel 100 kilometers to do your errands. Does it pay?/Is it convenient?	*Fai 100 chilometri per fare la spesa. Ma ti conviene?*
brand	la marca
brand new	nuovo di fabbrica
cheap	a buon mercato; conveniente; di bassa qualità
In that store they only sell cheap stuff.	*In quel negozio vendono solo roba di bassa qualità.*
cost	costare; il costo

Comprare e vendere

 Must-Know Tip

Quanto costa? and **Quanto costano?** translate to: *How much does it cost?* and *How much do these cost?* meaning: *What is the price of this item?* Similarly, **Quanto fa?** and **Quant'è?** translate to: *How much is it?* meaning: *How much do I owe for this item?*

dear/expensive	caro
discount	scontare; lo sconto
find	trovare
knockoff	l(a)'imitazione
They sell knockoffs of Rolex watches for 30 euros.	*Vendono dei Rolex di imitazione per 30 euro.*
liquidate	liquidare
look for/seek	cercare
made in	fabbricato in/made in
Made-in-Italy products are an important item in Italy's balance of trade.	*Il made-in-Italy è una voce importante della bilancia commerciale italiana.*
mass production	la produzione in serie

money	**i soldi/il denaro**
price	**il prezzo**
I'll let you have three boxes of oranges for the price of two.	*Le lascio tre cassette di arance al prezzo di due.*
purchase	**acquistare; l(o)'acquisto**
raise	**aumentare/alzare; l(o)'aumento**
retail	**al dettaglio; al minuto**
sale	**la vendita**
The dress by Prada, which was for sale for 1,200 euros in September, is now on sale for 600 euros.	*Il vestito di Prada che era in vendita a 1.200 euro a settembre adesso è in saldo a 600 euro.*
secondhand	**seconda mano**
He bought a secondhand car in mint condition.	*Ha comprato una macchina di seconda mano che sembra nuova di fabbrica.*
stock	**stoccare; il magazzino**
The titanium frames are back ordered, but we do have the plastic ones in stock.	*L'ordinativo delle montature in titanio è in arretrato, ma abbiamo quelle di plastica in magazzino.*
trademark	**il marchio [registrato]**
wholesale	**all(o)'ingrosso**
Prices double from wholesale to retail.	*I prezzi raddoppiano dall'ingrosso al minuto.*

Payments

I modi di pagamento

ATM card	**la cartina del bancomat; il bancomat**
cash	**incassare; il contante/i contanti**
My cousin is so rich that he pays for everything in cash.	*Mio cugino è così ricco che paga tutto in contanti.*
cashier	**il cassiere, la cassiera; i cassieri, le cassiere**
change	**cambiare; il resto; gli spiccioli**
I'm sorry, I've got no change left.	*Mi dispiace, sono rimasto senza spiccioli.*

check	controllare; il conto; l(o)'assegno
free	gratis/gratuito
For two weeks, entry to the museum is free.	*Per due settimane, l'ingresso al museo è gratis/gratuito.*
installments	le rate
You can buy this giant flat-screen TV in twenty-four installments!	*Potete comprare questa televisione gigante a schermo piatto in ventiquattro rate!*
invoice	fatturare; la fattura
receipt	la ricevuta; lo scontrino
VAT (value-added tax)	[l(a)'] IVA (imposta sul valore aggiunto)
Thanks to the tax-free provision, you get back the VAT when you take merchandise abroad.	*Grazie al tax free ti restituiscono l'importo dell'IVA sulle merci che porti all'estero.*

Customer Service

Il servizio alla clientela

carry	tenere; portare
Do you carry those shoes in black and brown only?	*Tiene quelle scarpe solo in marrone e in nero?*
It was too heavy to carry.	*Era troppo pesante da portare.*
client	il, la cliente
complain	reclamare
e-commerce	il commercio elettronico
hold	tenere da parte
merchandise	la merce
money back; reimbursement	il rimborso
order	ordinare; l(o)'ordine
return	rendere; la resa
salesperson	il commesso
satisfaction	la soddisfazione

Stores

I negozi

| appliance store | il negozio di elettrodomestici |
| bakery | la panetteria |

barber shop	**il barbiere**
beauty salon	**il salone di bellezza**
bookstore	**la libreria**
boutique	**la boutique**
chain	**incatenare; la catena**
cleaner's	**la tintoria/il lavasecco**
close	**chiudere**
closed	**chiuso**
Sorry, we're closed.	*Oggi chiuso.*
cosmetic/beauty products store	**la profumeria**
department store	**il grande magazzino**
drugstore	**il negozio di generi vari**
electronic store	**il negozio di elettronica**
escalator	**la scala mobile**
flower shop	**il fioraio; il, la fiorista; i fioristi, le fioriste**
furniture store	**il negozio di mobili/di arredamento**
grocery store	**la drogheria**
hairdresser's	*il parrucchiere, la parrucchiera; la pettinatrice* (fem. only)
hardware store	**il [negozio di] ferramenta**
housewares store	**il negozio di casalinghi; i casalinghi**
ice cream shop	**la gelateria**
market	**il mercato**
megastore	**l(o)'ipermercato**

open	**aprire; aperto**
music store	**il negozio di dischi**
Store hours are 9 A.M. to 1 P.M.,	***L'orario di apertura del negozio è***
and 3:30 P.M. to 7:30 P.M.	***dalle 9 alle 13, e dalle 15 e 30 alle***
	19 e 30.
pastry shop	**la pasticceria**
pharmacy	**la farmacia**
shopkeeper	**il, la negoziante**
shopping mall	**il centro commerciale**
stationery shop	**la cartoleria**
supermarket	**il supermarket/il supermercato**

Advertising — La pubblicità

advertisement	**la pubblicità/la reclame**
advertising professional	**il pubblicitario**
campaign	**la campagna [pubblicitaria]**
launch	**lanciare; il lancio**
logo	**il logo; il marchio**
marketing	**il marketing**
market share	**la quota di mercato**
market survey	**l(a)'indagine di mercato**
product	**il prodotto**
slogan	**lo slogan [pubblicitario]**
spot	**l(o)'annuncio; lo spot [pubblicitario]**

Colors — I colori

| beige | **[il] beige** |
| black | **[il] nero** |

 Must-Know Tip

In both Italian and English, we often use a pejorative to convey a faded or unpleasant hue: **nerastro** (*blackish*), **biancastro** (*whitish*), **giallastro** (*yellowish*), etc.

| *His skin is yellowish. In my* | ***Ha la pella giallastra. Secondo me*** |
| *opinion he isn't well.* | ***non sta bene.*** |

blue	**[il] blu**
brown	**[il] marrone**
burgundy	**[il] rosso scuro; [il] bordeaux**
gray	**[il] grigio**
green	**[il] verde**
That apple is green, but it's ripe.	***Questa mela è verde, ma è già matura.***
lilac	**[il] lilla; il lillà** (flower)
ocher	**[l(o)'] ocra**
off-white	**[il] bianco sporco/[l(o)'] écru**
orange	**[l(o)'] arancione**
pastel	**[il] pastello**
primary	**primario**
Red is a primary color; green is obtained by mixing blue and yellow.	***Il rosso è un colore primario, mentre il verde si ottiene mescolando il blu e il giallo.***
pink	**[il] rosa**
red	**[il] rosso**
FF *Do you prefer a red or a pink rose?*	***Preferisci una rosa rossa o una rosa?***
sky blue; azure	**[l(o)'] azzurro; [il] celeste**
turquoise	**[il] turchese**
violet	**[il] viola**
white	**[il] bianco**
yellow	**[il] giallo**
In Italy, Mondadori published the first murder mysteries with a yellow cover; since then they have been known as i gialli *(yellow novels).*	***In Italia, la Mondadori pubblicò i primi romanzi polizieschi con una copertina gialla, e da allora si chiamano 'i gialli'.***

Clothes

Clothing Store

Il negozio di abbigliamento

attire	**l(o)'abbigliamento**
button	**abbottonare; il bottone**
casual	**casual; casuale** (not used for clothes)

She likes to dress casual at work, too.	*Le piace vestirsi casual anche per andare a lavorare.*
It was a casual encounter.	*È stato un incontro casuale.*
dressing room	**il camerino**
elegant	**elegante**
garment/item of clothing	**il capo di vestiario**
hanger	**l(o)'attaccapanni**
haute couture	**l(a)'alta moda**
All the great names of the fashion industry will be at the haute couture shows in Paris.	*Tutte le grandi firme saranno alle sfilate dell'alta moda a Parigi.*
inside out	**al contrario/al rovescio**
look	**il look**
match	**intonarsi [con]; andare/stare bene insieme**
model	**il modello**
My sister is one of the highest-paid cover girls in the world.	*Mia sorella è una delle ragazze da copertina più pagate al mondo.*
runway	**la passerella**
size	**la taglia; la misura**

 Must-Know Tip

Italian uses **misura** for sizes of shoes and clothes, and **taglia** for clothes only.

My mother wears size 10 for clothes and size 7 for shoes. — *Mia madre porta la taglia 48 di vestiario, e la misura 38 di scarpe.*

Those pants are not my size. — *Quei pantaloni non sono della mia misura.*

---

sporty	**sportivo**
tacky	**volgare; di cattivo gusto**
tailor	**fare su misura; il sarto**
In Italy I still have a seamstress who custom-tailors clothes.	*In Italia ho ancora una sarta che mi fa gli abiti su misura.*

try on	provare/misurare
window	la vetrina
window dresser	il, la vetrinista; i vetrinisti, le vetriniste
Their window dresser makes the mannequins look like live people.	*La loro vetrinista ti dà l'illusione che i manichini siano persone in carne e ossa.*

Clothing / Il vestiario

cardigan; sweater	il golf; il cardigan; la maglia
[over]coat	il cappotto; il giaccone
cotton	il cotone
down coat	il piumone; l(o)'imbottito
dress	il vestito (da donna); l(o)'abito (da donna e da uomo); vestire; vestirsi
She got dressed and undressed in two minutes.	*Si è vestita e svestita in due minuti.*
She dressed up for New Year's Eve.	*Si è vestita tutta elegante per Capodanno.*
evening gown	l(o)'abito [da sera] lungo
fabric	la stoffa
fashion	la moda
Long skirts are out of fashion, but you'll see, they'll be back in fashion soon.	*Le gonne lunghe sono fuori moda, ma vedrai che torneranno di moda presto.*
fit	andar[e] bene
handmade	fatto a mano

 Must-Know Tip

Qualities and characteristics can be conveyed in Italian with the preposition **a** (*at, to*) followed by a noun: **a mano** (*by hand*), **a macchina** (*machine made*), **a fiori** (*with a floral pattern*), **a righe** (*striped*), **a quadretti** (*checkered*), **a pied-de-poule** (*hound's tooth*), **a pois** (*polka dots*), **a maglia** (*knitted*), **all'uncinetto** (*crochet*).

hem	l(o)'orlo
jacket	la giacca
[blue] jeans	i [blue] jeans
label; tag	etichettare; l(a)'etichetta
I can't find the price tag for this evening bag.	*Non vedo l'etichetta con il prezzo di questa borsetta da sera.*
lace	il pizzo
latest fad	l(o)'ultimo grido; l(a)'ultima moda
linen	il lino
maternity clothes	gli abiti premaman
microfiber	la microfibra
pants; slacks; trousers	i pantaloni
pattern	[la] fantasia
She only wears dresses with a pattern.	*Porta solo vestiti fantasia.*
pocket	la tasca
polyester	il poliestere
put on	mettersi [addosso]
raincoat	l(o)'impermeabile
rayon	il raion; la viscosa
shirt	la camicia; la camicetta (da donna)
shorts	i pantaloni corti
silk	la seta
skirt	la gonna
The miniskirt was launched by Mary Quant in the 1960s.	*La minigonna venne lanciata da Mary Quant negli anni sessanta.*
solid	[la] tinta unita
It's a beautiful fabric, but it only comes in solid colors.	*È una stoffa bellissima, ma la producono solo in tinta unita.*
stripe	la striscia; la riga
suit	essere adatto [a]; l(o)'abito da uomo; il tailleur (only for women)
That dress is beautiful, but it doesn't suit you.	*Quel vestito è bello, ma non è adatto a te.*
This suit is very expensive.	*Quest'abito da uomo è molto caro.*
sweatshirt	la felpa

take off	**togliersi [di dosso]**
tear	**strappare**
top	**il top**
T-shirt	**la T-shirt; la maglietta; la canottiera**
tuxedo	**lo smoking**
twin set	**i gemelli**
two-piece garment	**il completo; lo spezzato**
velvet	**[il] velluto**
vest	**il gilé/il panciotto**
wear	**portare; indossare**
wool	**la lana**
zipper	**la cerniera lampo/la zip**

Shoes, Leather Goods, and Accessories

Le calzature, i prodotti in pelle e gli accessori

bag	**la borsa**
belt	**la cintura**
boots	**gli stivali**
briefcase	**la cartella**
fur coat	**la pelliccia**
She has all kinds of fur coats.	*Ha pellicce di tutti i tipi.*
gloves	**i guanti**
hat	**il cappello**
purse/handbag	**la borsetta**
ribbon	**il nastro**
sandals	**i sandali**
scarf	**la sciarpa**
shawl	**lo scialle**
shoe	**la scarpa**
shoelaces	**i lacci [delle scarpe]**
slippers	**le pantofole**
spikes/stiletto heels	**i tacchi a spillo**
suede	**la renna; di renna; la pelle scamosciata**
tie	**legare; la cravatta**

| umbrella | l(o)'ombrello |
| wallet | il portafoglio, i portafogli |

Lingerie
La biancheria intima

bodice	il body; il busto
bra	il reggiseno
briefs/underpants	le mutande [da uomo]; le mutandine [da donna]
nightshirt	la camicia da notte
pajamas [pair of]	il pigiama, i pigiami
pantyhose	il collant
robe	la vestaglia

I gave my father a terrycloth robe for his birthday. — *Per il suo compleanno, a papà ho regalato una vestaglia di spugna.*

slip	la sottoveste
stockings	le calze
socks	i calzini
undershirt	la canottiera; la maglietta
underwear; lingerie	la biancheria intima; la lingerie

Jewelry
I gioielli

costume jewelry	la bigiotteria
diamond	il diamante; il brillante
earrings	gli orecchini
gold	l(o)'oro

Our goldsmith can work with silver, gold, platinum, and steel. — *Il nostro orafo lavora con l'argento, l'oro, il platino e l'acciaio.*

jewelry maker; jeweler	il gioielliere
necklace	la collana
pearls	le perle
pin/brooch	la spilla
precious stone	la pietra preziosa

What kind of precious stone do you prefer, Madam: ruby, emerald, topaz, or sapphire? — *Che pietra preziosa preferisce, Signora: il rubino, lo smeraldo, il topazio o lo zaffiro?*

| ring | l(o)'anello |

Food and Drinks

Beverages

Le bevande

after-dinner cordial	**il digestivo; il cordiale**
beer	**la birra**
brew [coffee, tea]	**preparare/fare [il caffè, il tè]**
Coca-Cola	**la Coca-cola/la Coca**
coffee	**il caffè; l'espresso**
decaffeinated	**decaffeinato**
fizzy/bubbly	**gassato**
ground	**macinato**
hot chocolate	**la cioccolata calda**
juice	**la spremuta; il succo**
liqueur	**il liquore**
loose	**sciolto**
He buys coffee loose, a quarter pound at a time.	*Compra il caffè sciolto, un etto per volta.*
mineral water	**l(a)'acqua minerale**
nonalcoholic beverage	**l(o)'analcolico**
sodas	**le bevande gassate**
spirits; alcoholic drink	**il liquore; la bevanda alcolica**
squeeze	**spremere**
tea	**il tè; la tisana**
wine	**il vino**

Bread, Pastries, and Sweets

Il pane, le paste e i dolci

baguette	**lo sfilatino**
breadsticks	**i grissini**
cake	**la torta**
candies	**le caramelle**
chocolates	**i cioccolatini**
cookies	**i biscotti**
Easter dove cake	**la colomba pasquale**
loaf	**la pagnotta**
pie; tart	**la crostata**
run out	**esaurire; rimanere senza**

The store ran out of stock.	*Il negozio ha esaurito le scorte.*
We ran out of bread.	*Siamo rimasti senza pane.*
toast	tostare; il pane tostato; il pan carré
whole wheat	integrale

Meat and Fish / La carne e il pesce

beef	il manzo
chicken	il pollo
He likes beef, not chicken.	*Gli piace il manzo, non il pollo.*
cod	il merluzzo
edible	mangiabile; commestibile
Are you sure that this meat is still edible?	*Sei sicura che questa carne sia ancora mangiabile?*
Those nuts aren't edible.	*Quelle noci non sono commestibili.*
expiration date	la scadenza
game	la cacciagione
hare	la lepre
lamb	l(o)'agnello
lobster	l(a)'aragosta
partridge	la pernice
pork	il maiale
quail	la quaglia
rabbit	il coniglio
sausage	la salsiccia
seafood; shellfish	i frutti di mare
shrimp	i gamberetti
swordfish	il pesce spada
trout	la trota
tuna	il tonno
turkey	il tacchino
veal	il vitello

At the Delicatessen / In salumeria e in rosticceria

bologna	la mortadella
catering service	i rinfreschi a domicilio; il catering

chicken roasted on a spit	**il pollo allo spiedo**
cold cuts	**gli affettati**
fresh pasta	**la pasta fresca/all(o)'uovo**
ham	**il prosciutto [cotto]**
home delivery	**la consegna a domicilio**
Russian salad	**l(a)'insalata russa**
olives	**le olive**
pickles	**i sottaceti**
prosciutto/raw ham	**il prosciutto [crudo]**
ravioli	**i ravioli**
salami	**il salame; i salami**
takeout	**da asporto**
Our deli doesn't have takeout pizza any longer.	***La nostra rosticceria non tiene più la pizza da asporto.***
tortelloni	**i tortelloni**

Fruits and Vegetables

La frutta e la verdura

salad; any leafy vegetable used in salad	**l(a)'insalata**
apple	**la mela**
apricot	**l(a)'albicocca**
artichoke	**il carciofo**
asparagus	**gli asparagi**
banana	**la banana**
basil	**il basilico**
beans	**i fagioli**
blueberries	**i mirtilli**
cabbage	**il cavolo**
carrot	**la carota**
celery	**il sedano**
cherry	**la ciliegia**
clementine	**il mandarino**
eggplant	**la melanzana**
farmers' market	**il mercato dei contadini**

fennel	**il finocchio**
fig	**il fico**
fresh	**fresco**
garlic	**l(o)'aglio**
grapefruit	**il pompelmo**
grape(s)	**l(a)'uva**
herbs	**le erbe**
lemon	**il limone**
lettuce	**la lattuga**
marjoram	**la maggiorana**
market stand	**la bancarella del mercato**
melon	**il melone**
mint	**la menta**
mushrooms	**i funghi**
onion	**la cipolla**
orange	**l(a)'arancia**
oregano	**l(o)'origano**
parsley	**il prezzemolo**
peach	**la pesca**
pear	**la pera**
peas	**i piselli**
pineapple	**l(o)'ananas**
potato	**la patata**
pumpkin	**la zucca**
ripe	**maturo**
rosemary	**il rosmarino**
rotten	**marcio**
sage	**la salvia**
spinach	**gli spinaci**
string beans	**i fagiolini**
strawberries	**le fragole**
sweet pepper	**il peperone**
thyme	**il timo**
tomato	**il pomodoro**

watermelon	l(a)'anguria
zucchini	gli zucchini

At the Grocery Store and Dairy

In drogheria e in latteria

bouillon cube	il dado [da brodo]
butter	il burro
canned food	il cibo in scatola
cheese	il formaggio
It's not real parmesan if it doesn't have the official certification mark.	*Non è vero parmigiano se non ha il marchio di origine.*
cornmeal	la farina gialla/da polenta
cream	la panna; la crema
I love whipped cream!	*Adoro la panna montata!*
dozen	la dozzina
For this recipe we need half a dozen eggs.	*Per questa ricetta ci vuole mezza dozzina di uova.*
I bought two dozen eggs.	*Ho comprato due dozzine di uova.*
egg	l(o)'uovo, le uova
flour	la farina
hot red pepper	il peperoncino rosso
ice cream	il gelato
mayonnaise	la maionese
milk	mungere; il latte
mustard	la senape
oil	l(o)'olio
peeled tomatoes	i [pomodori] pelati
pepper	il pepe
potato chips	le patatine [fritte]
I like fries, not chips.	*Mi piacciono le patate fritte, non le patatine.*
preserve	conservare; la conserva; la marmellata
rice	il riso

salt	**il sale**
spoil	**andare a male; guastarsi**
stock	**il brodo [di carne]**
sugar	**lo zucchero**
vegetable shortening	**lo strutto vegetale**
vinegar	**l(o)'aceto**

6

A Place to Live

Housing

Types of Housing and Surroundings

Abitazioni e zone

across	**attraverso; dall'altra parte**
The store you're looking for is across the street.	*Il negozio che cerca è dall'altra parte della strada.*
apartment	**l(o)'appartamento; l(o)'alloggio**
attic	**la mansarda; la soffitta** (mostly for storage)
I found an old photo album in the attic.	*Ho trovato un vecchio album di fotografie in soffitta.*
back	**il retro**
before; in front of	**davanti [a]**
There is a van parked on the lawn in front of the house!	*C'è un camioncino parcheggiato sul prato davanti a casa!*
behind	**dietro [a]**
building	**l(o)'edificio; il caseggiato** (apartment building)
close/near	**vicino [a]**
condominium	**il condominio**
cooperative	**la cooperativa [edilizia]**
downtown/city center	**[il] centro**
We finally managed to move downtown, after many years in the outskirts.	*Finalmente siamo riusciti a spostarci in centro, dopo tanti anni passati in periferia.*
dwelling	**l(a)'abitazione**
environs	**i dintorni**
estate	**la tenuta**
far [away from]	**lontano [da]**
farmhouse	**la cascina**
front (of house)	**il fronte**
home/house	**[la] casa**

in/inside	**dentro; al chiuso**
loft	**il loft; il soppalco**
mansion	**il villone; il maniero**
The upkeep of the mansion will cost you an arm and a leg.	***La manutenzione del villone ti costerà un occhio.***
metropolis	**la metropoli, le metropoli**
move	**traslocare; trasferirsi**
outside	**fuori; all'aperto**
palace	**il palazzo**
place	**il posto**

prefab[ricated]	**[il] prefabbricato**
projects	**le case popolari**
settle	**stabilirsi**
sidewalk	**il marciapiede**

single-family house	**la casa/villetta unifamigliare**
skyscraper	**il grattacielo**
slum; ghetto	**il ghetto**
studio	**il monolocale**
subsidized housing	**l(a)'edilizia agevolata**
suburbs	**i sobborghi**
town houses	**le case a schiera**
urban	**urbano**

Features and Fixtures

Caratteristiche e componenti della casa

air conditioning [system]	**l(a)'aria condizionata**
asbestos	**l(o)'asbesto**
balcony	**il balcone**
banister	**il mancorrente; la ringhiera**
basement	**il seminterrato**
Beware of the dog!	***Attenti al cane!***
burglar alarm	**il sistema di allarme/antifurto**
ceiling	**il soffitto**
cellar	**la cantina**
chimney	**il camino; la canna del camino**
courtyard	**il cortile**
door	**la porta; il portone**
Keep the door to the building locked at all times.	***Tieni sempre chiuso a chiave il portone.***
doorman/concierge	**il portinaio**
elevator	**l(o)'ascensore**
facade	**la facciata**
face	**guardare a/verso; affacciarsi su**
Her friend finally found a house that faces south.	***Finalmente la sua amica ha trovato una casa che guarda a sud.***
Her friend bought a beautiful villa facing the lake.	***La sua amica ha comprato una bella villa che si affaccia sul lago.***
fan	**il ventilatore; il ventaglio**
fence	**la staccionata; la cancellata**

We had to build a fence to prevent our neighbor's Doberman from entering our backyard.	*Abbiamo dovuto far costruire una cancellata per impedire al doberman dei vicini di entrare nel nostro giardino.*
fireplace	**il camino/il caminetto**
floor	**il pavimento; il piano**

Must-Know Tip

In Italy, what in the United States would be called the first floor is always called the ground floor: **il pianterreno** (sing. only). The next floor level is called the first floor: **il primo piano**, and so forth. The top floor is called **l'ultimo piano**.

We live on the third floor.	**Abitiamo al quarto piano.**
It's a three-story house.	**È una casa di tre piani.**

furnace	**la caldaia**
garage	**il garage**
gate	**il cancello**
generator	**il generatore**
handrail	**il mancorrente**
heating [system]	**il [sistema di] riscaldamento**
intercom	**il citofono**
key	**la chiave**
landing	**il pianerottolo**
lock	**chiudere a chiave; la serratura**
mantelpiece	**la mensola del caminetto**
meter	**il contatore**
mold	**la muffa**
radiator	**il radiatore; il termosifone**
railing	**la ringhiera**
roof	**il tetto**
roof tiles	**le tegole**
room	**la camera/la stanza**
shutter	**la persiana**

stairs	**le scale**
He climbs the stairs four steps at a time.	*Fa le scale quattro gradini alla volta.*
walk upstairs/downstairs	**salire le scale; scendere le scale; andare su/giù**
water heater	**lo scaldaacqua/il boiler**
window	**la finestra**

Buying, Selling, and Renting
La compravendita e l(o)'affitto

agency	**l(a)'agenzia**
Our real estate agent found a great penthouse for us at a good price.	*La nostra agente immobiliare ci ha trovato un bellissimo attico a un buon prezzo.*
bid	**fare un(a)'offerta; l(o)'offerta**
buy	**comprare**
commission	**la commissione**
deed/title transfer	**il rogito**
deposit	**la caparra; l(o)'acconto**
eviction	**lo sfratto**
inspection	**la perizia**
lease	**dare in affitto; il contratto d'affitto**
let	**dare in affitto; affittare**
location	**la posizione**
They bought a house in a beautiful location.	*Hanno comprato una casa in una bellissima posizione.*
mortgage	**ipotecare; il mutuo**
We went for a twenty-year mortgage with a fixed interest rate for the first five years and a variable rate afterward.	*Abbiamo scelto un mutuo ventennale con i primi cinque anni a tasso fisso e con tasso variabile dopo.*
own	**possedere; essere proprietario di**
owner	**il proprietario**
property	**la proprietà**
property tax	**la tassa sulla casa/sugli immobili**
real estate	**la proprietà immobiliare/gli immobili**

rent	affittare; l(o)'affitto
She lived in a rent-controlled flat for many years, but she was evicted a month ago.	*Ha vissuto in un appartamento con l'affitto bloccato per molti anni, ma un mese fa l'hanno sfrattata.*
renter/tenant	l(o)'affittuario/l(o)'inquilino
sell	vendere
sublet	subaffittare; il subaffitto
two-bedroom apartment	[il] bilocale
For rent: two-bedroom apartment with eat-in kitchen, private garage, and basement.	*Affittasi bilocale con cucina abitabile, garage privato e seminterrato.*
virtual tour	la visita virtuale

Construction, Repairs, and Remodeling — Le costruzioni, le riparazioni e le ristutturazioni

assemble	montare
build	costruire
The city will tear down all houses built without a building permit.	*Il comune farà abbattere tutte le case costruite senza il permesso edilizio.*
dig	scavare; lo scavo
drill	trapanare; il trapano
carpenter	il falegname (m&f)
construction site	il cantiere [edile]
contractor	l(o)'impresario [edile] (m&f)
crane	la gru
crooked	storto
electrical current	la corrente elettrica
electrician	l(o, a)'elettricista; gli elettricisti, le elettriciste
electricity	l(a)'elettricità
[civil] engineer	l'ingegnere [civile] (m&f)
foreman	il capocantiere (m&f)
foundations	le fondamenta
fuse	il fusibile
gadget	l(o)'arnese

gravel	la ghiaia
hammer	martellare; il martello
install	installare
lay	posare; mettere
leak	avere una perdita; la perdita
level	in piano; il livello
mason	il muratore (m&f)
mend; repair	aggiustare; riparare
nail	inchiodare; il chiodo
paint	pitturare/dipingere; la tinta
painter	il decoratore (m&f)/ l(o)'imbianchino
plumber	l(o)'idraulico
reinforced concrete	il cemento armato
saw	segare; la sega
screw	avvitare; la vite
screwdriver	il cacciavite
short circuit	il corto circuito
tile installer	il piastrellista
tool	l(o)'attrezzo
wall[s]	il muro; la muraglia; le mura
The Great Wall of China is 3,000 miles long.	*La Grande Muraglia cinese è lunga 5.000 chilometri.*

Rooms, Furniture, and Accessories

Furniture and Interior Decorating

I mobili e l'arredamento

antique[s]	l(o)'antiquariato; di antiquariato
[Venetian] blinds	le veneziane
bulb	la lampadina
candle	la candela
candlestick	il candeliere
carpet	la moquette

chandelier	il lampadario
curtain	la tenda
furnish	ammobiliare/arredare
Ever since they came out with modular furniture, furnishing a house has become much easier.	*Da quando hanno inventato i mobili componibili, arredare la casa è diventato molto più facile.*
furnished	ammobiliato/arredato
halogen	alogeno
lamp	la lampada
switch/turn on	accendere; aprire
switch/turn off	spegnere; chiudere
wallpaper	la tappezzeria

Hallway

L(o)'ingresso

[door]bell	il campanello
I rang the bell several times, but no one came to the door.	*Ho suonato il campanello a lungo, ma nessuno è venuto ad aprire.*
closet	lo sgabuzzino; il ripostiglio; l(o)'armadio a muro
coatrack/hook	l(o)'attaccapanni
doormat	lo zerbino
enter; come in	entrare
Come in!	*Avanti!*
go out	uscire
Did they all go out?	*Sono usciti tutti?*
After dinner we went out for a walk.	*Siamo usciti a fare una passeggiata dopo cena.*
knock	bussare
marble	il marmo
mirror	lo specchio

Bathroom

Il bagno

bathtub	la vasca [da bagno]
bidet	il bidè
faucet	il rubinetto

shower	**la doccia**
sink	**il lavabo**
sponge	**la spugna**
tiles	**le piastrelle**
toilet bowl	**la tazza del W.C.** (water closet)
toilet paper	**la carta igienica**
towel	**l(o)'asciugamano**

Bedroom — **La camera da letto**

alarm clock	**la sveglia**
bed	**il letto**
He goes to bed every evening at 9 P.M. sharp.	*Va a letto tutte le sere alle 9 in punto.*
blanket	**la coperta**
boxspring	**il pagliericcio**
chest of drawers; dresser	**la cassettiera/il cassettone**
comfort	**confortare; il confórt; i confórt/le comodità**
comfortable	**comodo**
get up	**alzarsi**
lie down	**coricarsi; distendersi**
mattress	**il materasso**
nap	**fare un sonnellino/pisolino; il sonnellino/pisolino**
night table	**il comodino [da notte]**
pillow	**il cuscino; il guanciale**
I was so tired I fell asleep as soon as my head hit the pillow.	*Ero così stanca che mi sono addormentata non appena ho posato la testa sul cuscino.*
pillowcase	**la federa**
quilt	**la trapunta**
sheets	**le lenzuola**
sleep	**dormire; il sonno**
wake [someone] up	**svegliare [qualcuno]; svegliarsi**
walk-in closet	**la cabina armadio**

Dining Room, Living Room, and Study

La sala da pranzo, il salotto e lo studio

armchair	**la poltrona**
ashtray	**il portacenere**
bookshelf	**lo scaffale; la libreria**
chair	**la sedia**
clear the table	**sparecchiare**
coffee table	**il tavolino**
cushion	**il cuscino**
grand room	**il salone**
hang	**appendere; stendere [la biancheria]**
We spent Sunday hanging paintings.	*Abbiamo passato la domenica ad appendere quadri.*
knickknacks	**i ninnoli; i soprammobili**
living room	**il soggiorno** (more formal, not necessarily with a dining area); **il tinello** (informal living and dining room)
mahagony	**il mogano**
rug	**il tappeto**
set the table	**apparecchiare**
sideboard	**la credenza**
sit	**sedersi; accomodarsi**
Please, take a seat.	*Prego, si accomodi.*
sofa	**il sofà/il divano**
stand up	**alzarsi [in piedi]**

 Must-Know Tip

The word **tavolo** refers to the piece of furniture people sit at, usually to eat. The word **tavola** means *board*. It is also used to signal functions performed at a table, as in the expression:

Come to the table. Dinner is served.   ***Venite a tavola! La cena è pronta.***

table	**il tavolo**
wood floor	**il parquet /il palchetto**

Kitchen — La cucina

cabinet	**l(o)'armadietto**
countertop	**il piano di lavoro**
Formica	**la fòrmica**
FF An ant is a hard-working insect.	*La formìca è un insetto molto laborioso.*
hanging cabinet	**il pensile**
kitchen sink	**il lavello**
kitchenette	**il cucinino**
pantry	**la dispensa**

Appliances — Gli elettrodomestici

coffee grinder	**il macinacaffè; i macinacaffè**
dishwasher	**il/la lavapiatti; il/la lavastoviglie**
drier	**l(o)'essicatore/l(o)'asciugatore**
food processor	**il tritatutto**
freezer	**il congelatore/il freezer**
garbage disposal	**il trituratore**
hood	**la cappa**
iron	**stirare; il ferro [da stiro]**
oven	**il forno**
I don't like cooking with the microwave oven.	*Non mi piace cucinare con il forno a microonde.*
range	**la cucina [a gas; elettrica]**
In our mountain cabin we have an old range fueled with a gas canister.	*Nello chalet in montagna abbiamo una vecchia cucina che funziona con una bombola a gas.*
refrigerator	**il frigorifero**
stove	**la stufa**
toaster	**il tostapane; i tostapane**
washing machine	**la [macchina] lavatrice**

Kitchen Tools

Gli utensili da cucina

baking dish	**la teglia da forno**
bottle	**la bottiglia**
bowl	**l(a)'insalatiera; la scodella**
can opener	**l(o)'apriscatole**
I asked you for the bottle opener, not the can opener.	*Ti ho chiesto l'apribottiglia, non l'apriscatole.*
carafe	**la caraffa**
colander	**il colapasta, i colapasta/lo scolapasta, gli scolapasta**
cork	**il tappo; il sughero**
corkscrew	**il cavatappi; i cavatappi**
cup	**la tazza; la tazzina**
cutting board	**il tagliere**
dishes/dinnerware	**i piatti**
It's so late. Let's do the dishes tomorrow morning.	*È così tardi! I piatti li possiamo fare domattina.*
fork	**la forchetta**
garbage	**l(a)'immondizia**
glass	**il bicchiere** (for drinking)**; il vetro** (window)
They gave her a beautiful glass set, with wine and water glasses.	*Le hanno regalato un bellissimo servizio di bicchieri da acqua e da vino.*
handle	**il manico**
knife	**il coltello**
ladle	**il mestolo**
lid	**il coperchio**
matches	**i fiammiferi**
mug	**il boccale**
napkin	**il tovagliolo**
pan	**la padella**
Some people say that Teflon pans are carcinogenic.	*C'è chi dice che le padelle antiaderenti di Teflon siano cancerogene.*
plate	**il piatto [piano]**

pot	**la pentola**
saucer	**il piattino**
soup bowl	**il piatto fondo**
spoon	**il cucchiaio**
tablecloth	**la tovaglia**
teapot	**la teiera**
teaspoon	**il cucchiaino**
tray	**il vassoio**

At Home

Meals

I pasti

appetizer	**l'antipasto**
breakfast	**la [prima] colazione**
course	**la portata**
dessert	**il dolce; il dessert**
dinner	**la cena**
fingerfood	**gli stuzzichini**
gluttony	**[la] gola**
gourmet	**il buongustaio**
leftovers	**gli avanzi**
What should we do with the leftovers?	*Che cosa dobbiamo farne degli avanzi?*
lunch	**il pranzo**
packed lunch	**la colazione al sacco**
picnic	**il picnic**
sandwich	**il panino/il sandwich**
sandwich (with toasted bread, ham, and cheese)	**il to[a]st**
serve	**servire**
service	**il servizio**
side dish	**il contorno**
snack	**lo spuntino/lo snack; la merenda** (mostly for kids)

Cooking at Home

bake

a cup of

1 pinch

1 tablespoon butter

1 teaspoon; 1 tablespoon

Cucinare a casa

cuocere al forno

una tazza di

un pizzico di

una noce di burro

un cucchiaino; un cucchiaio di

 Must-Know Tip

We can talk about activities linked to cooking by indicating the transformation occurring in the ingredients: **bollire** (*to boil*), **friggere** (*to fry*), **arrostire** (*to roast*); or the transformation the cook imparts to the ingredients: **far bollire** (*to bring to a boil*), **far friggere** (*to fry*), **far arrostire** (*to roast*).

The water is boiling. — ***L'acqua bolle.***

I'm bringing water to a boil. — ***Faccio bollire l'acqua.***

barbecue

be enough

Do you have enough butter?

That's enough!

Didn't you eat enough?

I've had enough!

boil

In Italy I'll have you try a truly typical dish: boiled meats.

broil

chop; mince

cook

cookbook

My grandmother wrote a cookbook with old family recipes.

cooked/done

He likes his pasta cooked al dente.

cuisine

il barbecue

bastare; essere abbastanza

Ti basta il burro?

Basta così!

Non hai mangiato abbastanza?

Ne ho avuto abbastanza!

bollire

In Italia ti faccio assaggiare un piatto davvero tipico: il bollito misto.

cuocere alla griglia

tritare

cuocere; il cuoco

il libro di ricette

Mia nonna ha scritto un libro con le ricette di famiglia.

cotto

Gli piace la pasta al dente.

la cucina

cut	**tagliare; il taglio**
dose	**la dose**
drain	**scolare**
dress	**condire**
dressing	**il condimento**
empty [out]	**vuotare; vuoto**
fill	**riempire**
full	**pieno**
frozen food(s)	**i surgelati**
fry	**friggere**
grill	**grigliare; la griglia**
hard; tough	**duro**
hunger	**la fame** (sing. only)
I'm so hungry!	*Ho una fame!*
ingredient	**l(o)'ingrediente**
lukewarm	**tiepido**
medium	**poco cotto; semicotto; semicrudo**
overdone	**stracotto; scotto**
peel	**pelare; la buccia/la pelle**
Do you like lemon peel in cakes?	*Ti piace la buccia del limone nelle torte?*
The skin of those peaches is like velvet.	*La pelle di quelle pesche è così vellutata!*
portion	**la porzione**
I don't want a large portion.	*Non voglio una porzione troppo abbondante.*
They serve generous portions.	*Servono porzioni abbondanti.*
pour	**versare**
precooked meal	**il cibo/pasto precotto**
prepare a meal	**far da mangiare**
rare	**al sangue**
recipe	**la ricetta**
sauce	**la salsa; il sugo**
sauté	**soffriggere**
sautéed chopped ingredients	**il soffritto**

stale	**raffermo**
His grandmother likes stale bread.	*A sua nonna piace il pane raffermo.*
steam	**cuocere al vapore; il vapore**
stir	**girare; mescolare**
stuffing	**il ripieno**
My husband makes Thanksgiving turkey with a delicious stuffing.	*Mio marito fa il tacchino a Thanksgiving con un ripieno delizioso.*
thaw/defrost	**scongelare**
thirst	**la sete** (sing. only)
Are you thirsty?	*Hai sete?*
warm up	**riscaldare**
well done	**ben cotto**

Housecleaning — La pulizia della casa

butler	**il maggiordomo**
broom	**la scopa**
clean	**pulire; pulito**
clothespins	**le mollette**
detergent	**il detersivo; il detergente**
dirty	**sporco**
dirty clothes	**la roba sporca**
do/make the bed	**[ri]fare il letto**
dust	**spolverare; la polvere**
housewife	**la casalinga**
laundry/washing	**il bucato**
maid	**la colf/la collaboratrice famigliare**
mop	**lo spazzettone**
polish	**lucidare; il lucido**
put in order/straighten up	**mettere in ordine**
Straighten up your room, otherwise no TV tonight.	*Metti in ordine la tua camera, se no stasera niente TV.*
rag (for cleaning)	**lo strofinaccio**
rinse	**[ri]sciacquare**
spring cleaning	**le pulizie di Pasqua**

sweep	**scopare**
vacuum	**passare l(o)'aspirapolvere; passare il battitappeto** (for wall-to-wall carpet)
wax	**dare la cera; la cera**
wring	**strizzare**

Outdoor Space

Lo spazio intorno alla casa

backyard/garden	**il giardino**
She transformed the entire backyard into a vegetable garden.	*Ha trasformato tutto il giardino in un orto.*
garden furniture	**i mobili da giardino**
lawn	**il prato**
lawn mower	**il tagliaerba; i tagliaerba**
mow [the lawn]	**tagliare [l(a)'erba]**
porch	**la veranda; il portico**
rocking chair	**la sedia a dondolo**
swimming pool	**la piscina**
teak	**il tek; di tek**
terrace	**la terrazza**

7

Occupations and the Business World

Occupational Fields, Training, and Working Conditions

Occupations in Service and Industry / Occupazioni nei servizi e nell'industria

accountant	il, la contabile; il ragioniere, la ragioniera; i ragioneri, le ragioniere
charge	dare l'incarico; l'incarico
cleaning crew	gli addetti alle pulizie
computer expert	l(o)'esperto di computer
consultant	il, la consulente
CPA	il, la commercialista; i commercialisti, le commercialiste
craftsman	l(o)'artigiano
day laborer	il lavoratore a giornata
engineer	l(o)'ingegnere (m&f)
expert	il perito (m&f)
flowchart	l(o)'organigramma
governing board/board of directors	il consiglio di amministrazione
handyman	il factotum
lab technician	il tecnico di laboratorio
manager	il direttore, la direttrice; il, la dirigente; il, la manager
managing director	l(o)'amministratore delegato (m&f)
office manager	il, la capufficio; i, le capufficio
person in charge of	l(o)'addetto a
public relations person	l(o)'addetto alle pubbliche relazioni
secretary	la segretaria (il segretario, less common)
security guard	la guardia giurata
self-employed professional	il libero professionista
self-employment	la libera professione
skill	la capacità/l(a)'abilità
She's a skilled worker.	*È un'operaia specializzata.*
social worker	l(o, a)'assistente sociale

software technician	il tecnico di software
statistician	l(o)'esperto di statistica
technician	il tecnico; il perito (m&f)
worker	il lavoratore, la lavoratrice; l'operaio

Looking for a Job / La ricerca del lavoro

age limit	il limite di età
apprentice	l(o, a)'apprendista; gli apprendisti, le apprendiste
apprenticeship	l(o)'apprendistato
He did his apprenticeship in a foreign firm.	*Ha fatto l'apprendistato in una ditta straniera.*
attitudinal test	il test attitudinale
career	la carriera
competent	competente
competition	il concorso
In Italy people are often hired through a test-based competition, especially in the public sector.	*In Italia si assume spesso tramite concorso, specialmente nel settore pubblico.*
duties	le mansioni
employ	impiegare; dare lavoro
employee	l(o)'impiegato; il, la dipendente
employer	il datore/la datrice di lavoro
employment	l(o)'impiego
exploit	sfruttare
exploitation	lo sfruttamento
The struggle against the exploitation of the working class was the central aim of socialism.	*La lotta contro lo sfruttamento della classe operaia era l'obiettivo principale del socialismo.*
full-time [job]	il [lavoro a] tempo pieno/il [lavoro] full-time
hire	assumere; l(a)'assunzione
honor	onorare; l(o)'onore; il riconoscimento
human resources	l(o)'ufficio personale
internship	lo stage

job	il mestiere; il lavoro
job advertisement	l(o)'annuncio di lavoro
job interview	il colloquio [di lavoro]/ l(a)'intervista
motivated	motivato
networking	il networking
opportunity	l(o)'opportunità/l(a)'occasione
part-time [job]	il [lavoro a] tempo parziale/il [lavoro] part-time
personal data/information	i dati personali
position	il posto di lavoro
His position at work is in jeopardy.	*Il suo posto di lavoro è in pericolo.*
qualification; competency	la qualifica; la competenza
recommendation	la raccomandazione
references	le referenze
résumé/CV	il curricolo/il curriculum vitae
Did you put your CV online?	*Hai messo il tuo CV online?*
seasonal	stagionale
staff	il personale
team	l(a)'équipe; il team
temporary job	il lavoro precario; il contratto a tempo determinato
unemployed	[il] disoccupato
unemployment	la disoccupazione
work	lavorare; il lavoro; l'opera
You have an interesting résumé, but you need more work experience.	*Il suo curricolo è interessante, ma ha bisogno di maggiore esperienza lavorativa.*
They published a new complete edition of Aristotle's works.	*Hanno pubblicato una nuova edizione di tutte le opere di Aristotele.*

Labor-Management Relations / Le relazioni lavoratori-azienda

absenteeism	l(o)'assenteismo
agreement	l(o)'accordo

at the office	**in ufficio**
at work	**al lavoro**
boss	**il principale** (m&f); **il boss** (m&f)
break	**l(o)'intervallo**
complaint	**la lamentela**
contract	**il contratto [di lavoro]**
Trade unions and the industry representatives signed the new national contract.	*I sindacati e la Confindustria hanno firmato il nuovo contratto nazionale.*
decrease	**diminuire; il calo**
downsize	**ridurre il personale**
fire	**licenziare**
flexibility	**la flessibilità**
immigrant worker	**il lavoratore extracomunitario**
increase	**aumentare; l(o)'aumento**
industrialists' association	**la Confindustria**
labor market	**il mercato del lavoro**
labor relations	**le relazioni sindacali**
Labor relations have become much worse in recent years.	*Le relazioni sindacali sono peggiorate molto negli ultimi anni.*
lockout	**la serrata**
management	**l(a)'amministrazione/il management**
meeting	**la riunione**
midlevel managers	**i quadri intermedi**
moonlighting	**il secondo lavoro**
negotiation; bargaining	**il negoziato; la trattativa**
on probation	**in prova**
overtime	**lo straordinario**
picket line	**il picchetto**
pink slip	**la notifica di licenziamento (il foglietto rosa)**
protest	**protestare; la protesta**
quit	**licenziarsi**
quota	**la quota**
The new bill sets stiff limits to the quota of foreign workers.	*La nuova legge fissa dei limiti molto rigidi alla quota di lavoratori stranieri.*

residency permit	il permesso di soggiorno
resignation	le dimissioni
scab	il crumiro
shift	il turno
My husband worked the night shift for thirty years.	Mio marito ha fatto il turno di notte per trent'anni.
strike	scioperare; lo sciopero
trade union	il sindacato; la confederazione sindacale
Trade union representatives were fired first.	I sindacalisti sono stati licenziati per primi.
voucher	il ticket
The café where we used to go for lunch no longer accepts the voucher paid by the firm.	Il caffè dove andavamo di solito a pranzo non accetta più il ticket della ditta.
working hours	l(o)'orario di lavoro

Rights, Compensations, and Benefits

Diritti, remunerazioni e benefici

allow	permettere
bonus	la gratifica
contributions	i contributi
deduction	la detrazione; la trattenuta
entitlements	i diritti acquisiti
fringe benefit	il beneficio aggiuntivo
health coverage	la mutua; l(a)'assistenza sanitaria
invalidity	l(a)'invalidità
IRA [account]	la pensione integrativa
In Italy, too, there are now IRA accounts.	Anche in Italia adesso ci sono le pensioni integrative.
leave	il congedo; l(a)'aspettativa
My cousin has been on maternity leave for a year.	Mia cugina è in aspettativa per maternità da un anno.
paycheck	la busta paga; le buste paga
permit	permettere; il permesso
I asked for permission to go to the doctor.	Ho chiesto un permesso per andare dal medico.

piecework	[il] cottimo
She does piecework; you can guess how much she makes.	Lavora a cottimo, ti puoi immaginare quanto guadagna.
promotion	la promozione
pension	la pensione
The surviving spouse is entitled to the deceased spouse's pension benefits.	Il coniuge che sopravvive ha diritto alla pensione di reversibilità.
retire	andare in pensione
retirement	la pensione
salary	lo stipendio
My (monthly) salary is 4,000 euros gross, but only 2,500 euros net.	Il mio stipendio (mensile) lordo è 4.000 euro, ma quello netto solo 2.500.
severance package	la buonuscita; la liquidazione
Social Security	l(o)'INPS (Istituto Nazionale della Previdenza Sociale)
stock option	la partecipazione azionaria
unemployment benefits	il sussidio di disoccupazione
vacation time	le ferie
I didn't take any vacation time last year.	Non ho preso le ferie l'anno scorso.
wage	il salario
work-related injury	l(o)'infortunio sul lavoro

Finance, Business, and the Economy

Finance

La finanza

analyst	l(o, a)'analista; gli analisti, le analiste
A famous financial analyst got into trouble because she was pushing the stock of a firm on the verge of bankruptcy.	Una famosa analista finanziaria è finita nei guai perché spingeva la gente a comprare i titoli di una società sull'orlo del fallimento.
bond	l'obbligazione; il titolo
For sure, investing in treasury bonds doesn't yield much.	Certo che investire in titoli di stato non rende molto.
business	gli affari/il business; l(a)'attività

My cousin started a new business.	***Mia cugina ha iniziato una nuova attività.***
capital	**il capitale; la capitale**
For your project you need someone willing to provide venture capital.	***Per il tuo progetto ci vuole un finanziatore che ti fornisca il capitale di rischio.***
The capital of Argentina is Buenos Aires.	***La capitale dell'Argentina è Buenos Aires.***
coupon	**la cedola**
crash/crack	**crollare; il crollo/il crac**
The crash of Wall Street on October 28, 1929, triggered the Great Depression.	***Il crollo di Wall Street del 28 ottobre 1929 scatenò la Grande Depressione.***
derivatives	**i derivati**
dividend	**il dividendo**
expenditures	**le uscite**
finance	**finanziare; la finanza**
financial manager	**il promotore finanziario, la promotrice finanziaria**
fundamentals	**i [fattori] fondamentali**
futures	**i futures**
holding	**la holding**
gain	**guadagnare; il guadagno**
index	**l(o)'indice**
insider trading	**l(o)'insider trading**
interest rate	**il tasso di interesse**
invest	**investire**
FF *The driver who ran him over didn't even stop.*	***L'automobilista che l'ha investito non si è neanche fermato.***
investment	**l(o)' investimento**
The manager of her investment fund was arrested.	***Il manager del suo fondo di investimento è stato arrestato.***
investor	**l(o)'investitore** (m&f)
performance	**la prestazione/la performance**
play the stock market	**giocare in borsa**
profit	**guadagnare; il profitto**

return; yield	rendere; il rendimento
rip-off	imbrogliare; l(o)'imbroglio
risk	rischiare; il rischio
share	condividere; l(a)'azione
share/stockholder	l(o, a)'azionista; gli azionisti, le azioniste
speculation	la speculazione
spread	lo scarto/lo spread
stakeholder	il portatore di interesse/lo stakeholder
stock	il capitale azionario; il titolo azionario
stock exchange	la borsa
stock exchange [list]	il listino di borsa; la Borsa [valori]
tax and customs police	la Guardia di Finanza
tax return	la dichiarazione dei redditi
trader	l(o, a)'agente di borsa
volatility	la volatilità

Banking / Le operazioni bancarie

accrue	maturare
advance	l(o)'anticipo
ATM	lo sportello del bancomat/il bancomat
balance	l'equilibrio; il saldo; la bilancia
What's the balance on my checking account?	*Qual è il saldo sul mio conto corrente?*
In just three years the balance of trade went from active to passive.	*In soli tre anni la bilancia commerciale è passata dall'attivo al passivo.*
bank	la banca
banker/teller	il bancario/l(o)'impiegato di banca
banknote	la banconota
bankruptcy	la bancarotta
be thrifty	fare economia
borrow	prendere a prestito

bounce a check	emettere un assegno in bianco
cent	il centesimo
credit	accreditare; l(o)'accredito; il credito
debit	addebitare
debt	il debito
I'm in debt up to my neck.	*Sono indebitato fino al collo.*
deposit	depositare; il deposito
due date; expiration date	la scadenza
endorse	girare
finance charges	gli interessi passivi
go bankrupt	andare in/fare bancarotta; fallire
Their firm went bankrupt.	*La loro azienda è fallita.*
in the black	in nero
in the red	in rosso
Her account balance is often in the red.	*Il saldo sul suo conto è spesso in rosso.*
line of credit	l(a)'apertura di credito
loan	imprestare/dare in prestito; chiedere/ prendere in prestito; il prestito
percentage	[la] percentuale
safe	la cassaforte
safe deposit box	la cassetta di sicurezza
save	risparmiare
savings	i risparmi
service charges	le spese tenuta conto
statement	l(o)'estratto conto
teller	l(o)'operatore, l(o)'operatrice di sportello
to the order of	a favore di
transaction	l(o)'operazione; la transazione
withdraw	prelevare
withdrawal	il prelievo

Currencies / Le valute

dollar	il dollaro
euro	l(o)'euro

Must-Know Tip

The names of most major currencies are the same in English and Italian:
yen, **peseta**, **peso**, **rand**, **rial**, etc.

exchange	cambiare; il cambio
exchange rate	il tasso di cambio [valutario]
franc	il franco
guilder	il fiorino
lira	la lira
peg	ancorare
Until recently, the yuan was pegged to the dollar.	*Fino a poco tempo fa, lo yuan era ancorato al dollaro.*
pound sterling	la sterlina [inglese]
ruble	il rublo
rupee	la rupia

Monetary Policy / La politica monetaria

budget	fare il bilancio preventivo; il bilancio/il budget
default	l(a)'inadempienza/la default
deficit	il disavanzo; il deficit
deflation	la deflazione
European Central Bank (ECB)	la Banca Centrale Europea (BCE)
Federal Reserve (bank)	la Federal Reserve
inflation	l(a)'inflazione
International Monetary Fund (IMF)	il Fondo Monetario Internazionale (FMI)
revenue	l(o)'introito fiscale
stagflation	la stagflazione
surplus	il surplus
World Bank	la Banca Mondiale

Economy / L(a)'economia

agenda	l(o)'ordine del giorno/l(a)'agenda
FF Have you seen my notebook?	*Hai visto la mia agenda?*

antitrust	l(o)'antitrust
assembly line	la catena di montaggio
Robots have replaced assembly line workers in almost all factories.	*I robot hanno sostituito gli operai alla catena di montaggio in quasi tutte le fabbriche.*
bid	la gara d'appalto; l(a)'offerta
boom	il boom
People remember with nostalgia the economic boom of the 1960s.	*La gente ricorda con nostalgia il boom economico degli anni sessanta.*
businessman; businesswoman	l'uomo d'affari; la donna d'affari
commerce	il commercio
company; firm	l(a)'azienda; la società; la ditta
We've finally become a public company.	*Finalmente siamo diventati una società quotata in borsa.*
competition	la concorrenza; la competizione
Competition is good for consumers.	*La concorrenza va al vantaggio del comsumatore.*
Luigi has been in competition with his brother ever since he was a kid.	*Luigi è stato in competizione con suo fratello fin da piccolo.*
competitive	competitivo
cooperative	la cooperativa
corporation	la società per azioni (S.p. A.)/la corporazione
costs	i costi
The costs of the merger have led us to conclude that it is too risky.	*Dall'analisi dei costi abbiamo concluso che la fusione è troppo rischiosa.*
crisis	la crisi/la congiuntura [negativa]
custom-built	fatto su ordinazione; fuori serie
demand	esigere; la domanda
development	lo sviluppo
earnings	i ricavi/gli utili; il fatturato
economic; economical	economico
The economic situation remains critical because of the war.	*La situazione economica resta grave a causa della guerra.*
I don't believe that hybrid cars are so economical in the end.	*Non credo che le automobili ibride siano poi così economiche.*

efficiency	l(a)'efficienza
entrepreneur	l(o)'imprenditore; l(a)'imprenditrice
exports	le esportazioni
factory	la fabbrica
foundation	la fondazione
franchising	il franchising
goods	i beni
Gross Domestic Product (GDP)	[il] Prodotto Interno Lordo (PIL)
growth	la crescita
headquarters	la sede [centrale]
imports	le importazioni
incentives	gli incentivi
income	il reddito; le entrate
In China yearly per capita income rose 6.5 percent from 1999 to 2000.	*In Cina il reddito anuale pro capite è salito del 6,5 per cento dal 1999 al 2000.*
industrialization	l(a)'industrializzazione
infrastructure	l(a)'infrastruttura
intellectual property	la proprietà intellettuale
manage	gestire
management	la direzione; la gestione; il management
manufacturing	il settore manifatturiero
mechanical	meccanico
monopoly	il monopolio
multinational	[la] multinazionale
necessary	necessario
A car is necessary if you live in the suburbs.	*L'automobile è necessaria se vivi fuori città.*
NGO (nongovernmental organization)	l(a)'ONG (Organizzazione Non Governativa)
not-for-profit	no-profit/nonprofit
In addition to the private and public sectors, people now refer to not-for-profits as the third sector.	*Oltre al settore privato e a quello pubblico, si parla adesso del nonprofit come del 'terzo settore'.*
patent	brevettare; il brevetto

privatization	la privatizzazione
poor	[il] povero
poverty	la povertà
produce	produrre
product	il prodotto
productivity	la produttività
pros and cons	il pro e il contro; i pro e i contro
raw materials	le materie prime
recession	la recessione
recovery	la ripresa
redistribution	la ridistribuzione
Research & Development	[la] Ricerca e [lo] Sviluppo
reserves	le riserve
resources	le risorse
rich	[il] ricco
rubber	la gomma
ruined	rovinato
structure	la struttura
supply	fornire; l(a)'offerta
tax exempt	esentasse
underdevelopment	il sottosviluppo
underground economy	l(a)'economia sommersa
Economists say that about 20 percent of Italian GDP comes from underground labor.	*Gli economisti sostengono che si deve circa il 20 per cento del PIL italiano al lavoro nero.*
use	usare
useful	utile
useless	inutile
wealth	la ricchezza
well-off	benestante

8

Leisure Time

Free Time and Entertainment

Circuses and Amusement Parks	I circhi [equestri] e i parchi dei divertimenti (il luna park)
acrobat	l(o, a)'acrobata; gli acrobati, le acrobate
clown	il pagliaccio (m&f), la pagliaccia (rare)
enjoy oneself	divertirsi
We enjoyed ourselves a lot at Disney World.	*Ci siamo divertiti un sacco a Disney World.*
juggler	il giocoliere (m&f)
knife thrower	il lanciatore, la lanciatrice di coltelli
leisure time	il tempo libero
lion tamer	il domatore, la domatrice
merry-go-round	la giostra
roller coaster	l(o)'ottovolante; la montagne russe
shooting gallery	il tiro a segno
showman	l(o)'uomo di spettacolo
tightrope walker	il funambolo
zoo	lo zoo; il giardino zoologico

Discos and Nightclubs	La discoteca e il night club
ballroom dancing	il ballo liscio
DJ/disc jockey	il, la DJ/il, la disc jockey

 Must-Know Tip

Italian uses the construction **andare a/stare andando a** + verb in the infinitive when English says *go* + verb in the gerund.

I'm going dancing tomorrow night.	***Vado a ballare domani sera.***
Are you going skiing?	***Stai andando a sciare?***
They want to go swimming.	***Vogliono andare a nuotare.***

follow	**seguire**
lead	**condurre**
microphone	**il microfono**
waltz	**il valzer**

Arts and Culture

Music

La musica

band	**il gruppo; la banda**
blues	**[il] blues**
choir; chorus	**il coro**
chord	**l(o)'accordo**
classic/classical	**[il] classico**
composer	**il compositore** (m&f)**; la compositrice** (rare)
concert	**il concerto**
conductor	**il direttore d'orchestra** (m&f)
country	**il country**
creative	**creativo**
encore	**il bis**
folk	**fokloristico**
heavy metal	**l(o)'heavy metal**
in tune	**intonato**
jazz	**il jazz**
key	**la chiave**
lyrics	**i versi [di un pezzo musicale]**
musical	**la commedia musicale/ il musical**
musician	**il, la musicista; i musicisti, le musiciste**
note	**annotare; notare; la nota**
opera	**l(o)'opera**
The most famous operettas are by Lehar.	*Le operette più famose sono quelle di Lehar.*

orchestra	l(a)'orchestra
out of tune	stonato
performance	l(a)'esecuzione/la performance
pop(ular)	pop/popolare
record	registrare; il disco

 Must-Know Tip

Italian uses the acronyms **CD** and **DVD**, using Italian pronunciation: **il Chee Dee, il Dee Vee Dee.**

refrain	il ritornello
rhythm	il ritmo
rock [and roll]	il rock [and roll]
sing	cantare
singer	il, la cantante
song	la canzone
[musical] staff	il pentagramma
symphony	la sinfonia
tone	il tono
tune	il motivo [musicale]
voice	la voce

Musical Instruments and Musicians
Gli strumenti musicali e i musicisti

accordion	la fisarmonica
bass, double bass	il contrabbasso
cello	il violoncello
clarinet	il clarinetto
drums	la batteria
flute	il flauto
guitar	la chitarra
keyboard	la tastiera
music stand	il leggio

organ	l(o)'organo
percussion	la percussione; a percussione
piano[forte]	il piano[forte]

 Must-Know Tip

Nouns indicating players of musical instruments are constructed by adding the suffix **-ista** in Italian, and *-ist* in English: **piano** → **[il, la] pianista**, **violino** → **[il, la] violinista**, etc. At times, Italian prefers the phrase **il suonatore di trombone, contrabbasso**, etc., even though **trombonista** (*trombonist*) and **contrabbassista** (*bass player*) do exist.

play	suonare
Do you play the bassoon?	*Suoni il fagotto?*
player	il suonatore, la suonatrice; il giocatore, la giocatrice
saxophone	il sassofono
score	lo spartito
soundtrack	la colonna sonora (del film)
stringed	a corda
trombone	il trombone
trumpet	la tromba
viola	la viola
violin	il violino
wind	a fiato

Ballet — Il balletto

ballerina	la ballerina
ballet company	il corpo di ballo
ballet shoes	le scarpette a punta
choreographer	il coreografo
dance	danzare; la danza; ballare
dancer	il ballerino
tutu	il tutù

Cinema and Theater	Il cinema e il teatro
act	recitare
actor	l(o)'attore, l(a)'attrice
applaud	applaudire
applause	l(o)'applauso
audience	il pubblico
boo	fischiare
The audience booed at his performance.	**Il pubblico lo ha fischiato.**
cartoons	i cartoni animati
cast	il cast
comedy	la commedia
costume	il costume
credits	i titoli [di testa/di coda]
curtain	il sipario
director	il, la regista; i registi, le registe
He won the Palme d'Or for best director at the Cannes Film Festival.	*Ha vinto la Palma d'oro per la regia al Festival di Cannes.*
documentary	il documentario
drama	il dramma
dress rehearsal	la prova generale
dub	doppiare
editing	il montaggio
end; ending	la fine
If you're depressed, why don't you go see a movie with a nice happy ending?	*Se sei depressa, perché non vai a vederti un film con un bel lieto fine?*
famous	famoso
film	filmare; il film
image	l(a)'immagine
The senator hired a media expert to hone his public image.	*Il senatore ha assunto un esperto di media che curi la sua immagine pubblica.*
intermission	l(o)'intervallo
mask	mascherare; la maschera
multiplex	la multisala
opening night	la sera della prima

protagonist	il, la protagonista; i protagonisti, le protagoniste
puppets	le marionette; i burattini
rehearsal	la prova
represent	rappresentare
representation	la rappresentazione
script	la sceneggiatura
shoot	girare
Did they finish shooting the movie?	*Hanno finito di girare il film?*
stage	il palcoscenico
star	la star, le star (f&m); la stella (f&m); il divo
subtitles	i sottotitoli
suspense	la suspense
theater	il teatro
[movie] theater	il cinema [tografo]
tragedy	la tragedia
trailer	il prossimamente; i prossimamente

Photography / La fotografia

background	lo sfondo; il background
black-and-white	il bianco e nero; in bianco e nero
camera	la macchina fotografica; la cinepresa
close-up; foreground	il primo piano; in primo piano
Richard Avedon was famous for his close-ups.	*Richard Avedon era famoso per i suoi primi piani.*
Why did you put that broken vase in the foreground?	*Perché hai messo quel vaso rotto in primo piano?*
dark room	la camera oscura
digital	digitale
flash	il flash
lens	la lente
negative	il negativo
photographer	il fotografo
projector	il proiettore

roll of film	il rullino
slide	la diapositiva
The slide show of her trip was a bit boring.	*La proiezione di diapositive del suo viaggio era un po' noiosa.*
zoom	zoomare; lo zoom

Television and Radio — La televisione e la radio

be on the air	essere in onda
broadcast	trasmettere; mandare in onda
cable	il cavo; via cavo
cassette	la cassetta
happen	succedere
What happened?	*Che cosa è successo?*
hit; success	[il] successo
host; anchor	il conduttore, la conduttrice; il presentatore, la presentatria
listener	l(o)'ascoltatore, l(a)'ascoltatrice
live	dal vivo
[mass] media	i [mass] media
network	la rete
participant	il, la concorrente; il, la partecipante
program	programmare; il programma
quiz	il quiz
radio/TV news	il giornale radio; il telegiornale/ il TG
remote control	il telecomando
satellite dish	la [antenna] parabolica
show	lo spettacolo/lo show
soap opera	la soap opera
sportscaster	il, la radiocronista [sportivo, a]; i radiocronisti, le radiocroniste; il, la telecronista; i telecronisti, le telecroniste
station	la stazione
television set	la televisione; il televisore; la TV

Painting

La pittura

abstract	**astratto**
artist	**l(o, a)'artista; gli artisti, le artiste**
auction	**l(a)'asta**
brush	**il pennello**
easel	**il cavalletto**
engraving	**l(a)'incisione**
exhibit	**esibire; la mostra**
fake	**[il] falso**
fine arts	**le belle arti**
frame	**incorniciare; la cornice**
fresco	**l(o)'affresco**
[art] gallery	**la galleria [d'arte]**
FF It's mandatory to turn on your beams in a tunnel.	*È obbligatorio accendere i fari in galleria.*
graffiti	**i graffiti**
graphic designer	**il grafico**
Have you ever thought of being a graphic designer?	*Hai mai pensato di fare il grafico?*
ink	**l(o)'inchiostro**
landscape	**il paesaggio**
mural	**il murale, i murali**
museum	**il museo**
naturalistic	**naturalista**
nude	**il nudo**
oil	**l(o)'olio; ad olio**
She does oil, tempera, and watercolor painting.	*Dipinge ad olio, a tempera e ad acquerello.*
paint	**dipingere; pitturare; la pittura**
painter	**il pittore, la pittrice**
painting	**il quadro**
palette	**la tavolozza; la gamma [dei colori]**
perspective	**la prospettiva**
portrait	**il ritratto**

pose	posare; la posa
FF She puts on airs.	*È una che posa.*
restoration	il restauro
self-portrait	l(o)'autoritratto
sponsor	sponsorizzare; lo sponsor
still life	la natura morta

Architecture — L(a)'architettura

architect	l(o)'architetto (m&f), l(a)'architetta (rare)
art nouveau	[il] liberty
baroque	[il] barocco
design	progettare; il progetto; il design
draw	disegnare
gothic	[il] gotico
model	modellare; il modello; il plastico
She was such a beautiful girl that she became a model for Vogue.	*Era una gran bella ragazza, infatti ha fatto la modella per* Vogue.
The planning commission wanted to see a model of our building before giving us the building permit.	*La commissione edilizia ci ha obbligato a presentare un plastico prima di darci il permesso edilizio.*
modern/modernist	[il] moderno
monument	il monumento
postmodern	[il] postmoderno
Renaissance style	lo stile rinascimentale; il Rinascimento
Romanesque	[il] romanico

Pottery and Sculpture — La ceramica e la scultura

bake; fire	cuocere [al forno]
bas-relief	il bassorilievo
bronze	il bronzo

carve	**intagliare**
clay	**l(a)'argilla**
dry	**essicare; far asciugare**
fusion	**la fusione**
mold	**lo stampo**
porcelain	**la porcellana**
potter	**il vasaio** (m&f)
sculptor	**lo scultore, la scultrice**
statue	**la statua**
vase	**il vaso**
wheel	**la ruota**

Reading

Literature

La letteratura

alphabet	**l(o)'alfabeto**
critic	**il critico** (m&f)
describe	**descrivere**
description	**la descrizione**
diary	**il diario**
fiction	**la narrativa/la fiction**
fictional	**di fantasia; fantastico**
Orson Welles's radio broadcast of Martians landing on earth was completely fictional.	***La radiocronaca di Orson Welles sull'arrivo dei marziani sulla terra era tutta di fantasia.***
illiterate	**[l(o/a)'] analfabeta**
He's illiterate.	***È analfabeta.***

novel	**il romanzo**
novelist	**il romanziere**
poem	**la poesia; il poema**
The Odyssey *is a great epic poem.*	**L'Odissea** *è un grande poema epico.*
poet	**il poeta, la poetessa**
poetry	**la poesia**
prose	**la prosa**
I love poetry more than prose.	*Mi piace la poesia più della prosa.*
read	**leggere**
reader	**il lettore, la lettrice**
realism	**il realismo**
review	**recensire; la recensione**
rhyme	**la rima**
satire	**la satira**
story	**la storia**
FF *Don't they teach you history in school any longer?*	*Ma non vi insegnano più la storia a scuola?*
tell	**raccontare [a]; dire [a]**
verse	**il verso**
writer	**lo scrittore, la scrittrice**

Books and Publishing

I libri e l'editoria

author	**l(o)'autore, l(a)'autrice**
citation	**la citazione**
cite	**citare**
conclude	**concludere**
conclusion	**[la] conclusione**
cover	**coprire; la copertina**
edited by	**a cura di**
edition	**l(a)'edizione**
editor	**il redattore, la redattrice; l(o)'editor (m&f)**
Without my editor's help I could never have finished my book.	*Senza l'aiuto del mio redattore non sarei mai riuscita a finire il libro.*
I have an excellent copyeditor.	*Ho un editor bravissimo.*
footnote	**la nota**

galleys; proofs	le bozze
It took me ten days to correct the proofs of my book.	*Ci ho messo dieci giorni a correggere le bozze del mio libro.*
in print	in stampa
murder mystery	il [libro/romanzo] giallo
out of print	esaurito
Are you sure this book is out of print?	*È sicuro che questo libro sia esaurito?*
paperback	il paperback
print	stampare; la stampa
publish	pubblicare
publisher	l(o)'editore (m&f)
She's been an important publisher for twenty years.	*È un editore importante da vent'anni.*
publishing house	la casa editrice
royalties	i diritti d'autore
table of contents	l(o)'indice [delle materie]
title	intitolare; il titolo

Press / La stampa

caption	la didascalia
circulation	la tiratura
current affairs	l(a)'attualità
editorial	l(o)'editoriale
front page	la prima pagina
They put the correction of that false news report on the back page.	*Hanno bubblicato la ritrattazione della notizia falsa in ultima pagina.*
headline	il titolo
interview	intervistare; l(a)'intervista
journalist	il, la giornalista; i giornalisti, le giornaliste
magazine	la rivista; il rotocalco
The new magazine, is it a weekly or a monthly?	*La nuova rivista, è un settimanale o un mensile?*
masthead	la testata
news	la notizia/le notizie

newspaper	il giornale; il quotidiano
newsstand	l(a)'edicola
press agency	l(a)'agenzia di stampa
report	dare notizia di; il rapporto
They never reported that the killer was the prime minister's son-in-law.	*Non hanno mai dato la notizia che l'assassino era il genero del primo ministro.*
scoop	il colpo giornalistico/lo scoop
section	l(o)'inserto
sensational	sensazionale
subscribe [to]	abbonarsi [a]
subscription	l(o)'abbonamento

Physical Activity and Equipment

Physical Exercise — L'esercizio fisico

aerobics	l(a)'aerobica
body building	il body building; il culturismo
exercise gear	l(a)'attrezzatura [sportiva]
fitness	la fitness; la forma
floor mat	il tappetino
gym	la palestra
gym clothes; tracksuit	la tuta da ginnastica
jog	fare jogging
personal trainer	l(o)'allenatore, l(o)'allenatrice personale
sneakers	le scarpe da ginnastica; le sneakers
stationary bike	la cyclette
weights	i pesi
work out; do exercises	fare ginnastica

Sports — Gli sport

amateur	[il, la] dilettante
athlete	l(o, a)'atleta; gli atleti, le atlete
athletics	l(a)'atletica [leggera]

bicycle	**la bici[cletta]**
biking/cycling	**il ciclismo**
boxer	**il pugile** (m&f)
boxing	**il pugilato/la box**
The trainer hasn't set foot in the ring ever since his favorite boxer died after a bout.	*Da quando il suo pugile preferito è morto dopo un match, l'allenatore non ha più messo piede sul ring.*
champion	**il campione, la campionessa**
cross-country skiing	**lo sci da fondo/il fondo**
cyclist	**il, la ciclista; i ciclisti, le cicliste**
dive	**tuffarsi; il tuffo**
doping	**il doping**
downhill/Alpine skiing	**lo sci da discesa/alpino**
extreme	**estremo**
final	**la finale**
finishing line	**il traguardo; il filo di lana**
He went through the finishing line in 9.5 seconds.	*Ha tagliato il traguardo in 9 secondi e mezzo.*
flame; torch	**la fiamma; la fiaccola**
gymnast	**il, la ginnasta; i ginnasti, le ginnaste**
gymnastics	**la ginnastica**
horseback riding	**l(a)'equitazione/andare a cavallo**
horse rider	**il cavallerizzo**
KO (knock out)	**il ko (cappa o)**
lap	**doppiare; l(o)'anello**
life jacket	**il salvagente**
lose	**perdere**
loser	**[il, la] perdente; lo sconfitto**
What a loser!	*È un perdente.*
medal	**la medaglia**
motorbike	**la moto[cicletta]**
Olympic games	**i giochi olimpici/le Olimpiadi**
Ping-Pong; table tennis	**il ping-pong; il tennis da tavolo**
place	**classificarsi; il posto [in classifica]**
placement/classification	**la classifica**

professional	**[il, la] professionista**
race	**gareggiare; la gara**
racquet	**la racchetta**
record	**il record**
run	**correre; la corsa**
sail	**fare vela; la vela**
The storm came up suddenly; we didn't even have time to lower the sails.	***La tempesta sopraggiunse così improvvisamente da non darci neanche il tempo di ammainare le vele.***
sailboat	**la barca a vela**
sailor	**il marinaio** (m&f) **/il, la velista; i velisti**
service	**il servizio**
skate	**pattinare; il pattino**
skater	**il pattinatore; la pattinatrice**
ski(s)	**sciare; gli sci**
I learned to ski without ski poles.	***Ho imparato a sciare senza bastoncini.***
skier	**lo sciatore, la sciatrice**
sportsman, sportswoman	**[lo] sportivo**
He's a true sportsman.	***È un vero sportivo.***
FF He's a little too glib for my taste.	***È un tipo un po' troppo sportivo per i miei gusti.***
swim	**nuotare**
swimmer	**il nuotatore; la nuotatrice**
tennis	**il tennis**
tennis court	**il campo da tennis**
tennis player	**il, la tennista; i tennisti, le tenniste**

 Must-Know Tip

Great Britain has given us many modern sports and their terminologies: **sport**, **football**, **tennis**, etc. In the case of tennis, **match**, **game**, and **set** remain unchanged in Italian. Scoring is translated as **15**, **30**, **40 a zero** (*15, 30, 40 love*), **parità** (*deuce*), and **vantaggio** (*advantage*).

tie	**fare pari; la parità; il pareggio**
trampoline	**il trampolino**
triumph	**trionfare; il trionfo**
trophy	**il trofeo**
victory	**la vittoria**
weight lifting	**il sollevamento pesi**
win	**vincere**
windsurfing	**il wind surfing**
winner	**il vincitore, la vincitrice**
wrestling	**la lotta (libera)**

Team Sports   Gli sport di squadra

ball	**il pallone; la palla; la pallina; la boccia**

Must-Know Tip

In order to specify for what game a ball is used, in many cases Italian uses the construction **la palla da.** For example, **il pallone da calcio** (*soccer ball*), **la pallina da tennis** (*tennis ball*), **la pallina da golf** (*golf ball*), etc.

baseball	**il baseball**
basket	**il cesto/il canestro**
basketball	**la pallacanestro/il basketball**

Must-Know Tip

There are nouns indicating the players of several sports or games: **il nuotatore** (*swimmer*), **lo sciatore** (*skier*), **il ciclista** (*cyclist*), etc. For other sports, we can, or have to use a phrase: **il giocatore di tennis/il, la tennista** (*tennis player*); **il giocatore di golf/il, la golfista** (*golfer*), **il giocatore di basket** (*basketball player*); **il giocatore di pallavolo/il, la pallavolista** (*volleyball player*); etc.

championship	**il campionato; lo scudetto**
coach	**l(o)'allenatore, l(a)'allenatrice**

In Italy, the coach of a soccer team is also called Mister.	In Italia l'allenatore di una squadra di calcio viene anche detto il Mister.
diamond	il diamante
fan	il fan (m&f); il tifoso
football	il football americano
foul	il fallo
game/match	la partita
glove/mitt	il guantone (da baseball)
goal (score)	la porta; la rete [in soccer]; il gol
He scored five goals in one game.	Ha fatto cinque gol in una partita.
hooligan	il, la teppista; l(o)'ultrà, gli ultrà
home run	il giro delle basi
league	la lega
The two main divisions of Italian soccer are division A and division B.	Le due divisioni più importanti del calcio italiano sono la serie A e la serie B.
kick	calciare; il calcio
penalty kick	il rigore
The goalkeeper didn't block the penalty kick.	Il portiere non è riuscito a parare il rigore.
referee/umpire	l(o)'arbitro (m&f)
relay	[la] staffetta
score	segnare; il punteggio
soccer	il calcio/il football
The Italian national soccer team is known as the Azzurri because of the color of their jerseys.	La squadra nazionale italiana di calcio è nota come 'gli Azzurri' dal colore della maglia.
soccer pools	il totocalcio; la schedina del totocalcio
My father did the soccer pools every week for thirty years without winning even one time.	Mio padre ha fatto la schedina del totocalcio ogni settimana per trent'anni, senza vincere neanche una volta.
stadium	lo stadio

tournament	**il torneo**
volleyball	**la pallavolo**

Pastimes/Hobbies — I passatempi/gli hobby

aim	**mirare; la mira**
bait	**l(a)'esca**
binoculars	**il binocolo**
bird-watching	**il bird-watching**
bullet	**la pallottola**
bull's eye	**il centro del bersaglio**
cartridge	**la cartuccia**
collect	**collezionare**
collector	**il collezionista**
crochet	**l(o)'uncinetto**
fish	**pescare; il pesce**
fisherman/angler	**il pescatore**
fishing	**la pesca**
fishing rod	**la canna da pesca**
game	**la cacciagione; il gioco; la partita**
I'm game.	*Ci sto./Sono della partita.*
hook	**l(o)'amo** (for fishing); **l(o)'uncinetto** (for crochet)
hunt	**cacciare**
hunter	**il cacciatore, la cacciatrice**
Big game hunting is a hobby for expert hunters.	*La caccia grossa è un hobby per cacciatori esperti.*
knit	**lavorare a maglia; fare la maglia**
line	**la lenza** (for fishing)
loom	**il telaio**
needle	**l(o)'ago; il ferro da calza**
Mom can no longer thread the needle.	*La mamma non riesce più a infilare l'ago.*
needlework/embroidery	**il ricamo**
prey	**la preda**
rifle	**il fucile**

sewing	il cucito
shoot	sparare
shot	lo sparo
target	il bersaglio
thread	il filo
weaving	la tessitura

Games and Puzzles — I giochi e l'enigmistica

anagram	l(o)'anagramma
bet	scommettere; puntare; la puntata
bluff	bluffare; il bluff
casino	il casinò
In one night, they lost 10,000 euros at the casino in Monte Carlo.	*Hanno perso 10.000 euro in una sera al casinò di Monte Carlo.*
FF *Kids, stop making such a racket!*	*Ragazzi, smettetela di piantare casino!*
charade	la sciarada
cheat	barare; il baro
checkers	la dama
checkmate	dare scacco matto a
In 1997 the computer Deeper Blue checkmated Grandmaster Kasparov.	*Nel 1997, il computer Deeper Blue diede scacco matto al gran maestro Kasparov.*
chess	gli scacchi
crossword puzzle	il cruciverba; le parole [in]crociate
deal the cards	dare le carte
dealer	il croupier (m&f)
deck	il mazzo
Did you cut the deck?	*Hai tagliato il mazzo?*
dice	i dadi
gamble	giocare d'azzardo
gambler	il giocatore, la giocatrice d(i)'azzardo
jigsaw puzzle	il puzzle
luck	la fortuna

lucky	**fortunato**
He's lucky at baccarat, but unlucky with slot machines.	*È molto fortunato a baccarat, ma sfortunato con le slot machine.*
magician	**il mago**
playing cards	**le carte [da gioco]**
pun	**il gioco di parole**
riddle	**l(o)'indovinello**

9

Transportation, Traffic, and Tourism

Transportation, Cars, and Traffic

Metropolitan and Suburban Transportation	I trasporti urbani e suburbani
away	via
Are you going away?	*Stai andando via?*
-bound	in direzione...
If you want to get to Palazzo Borghese, take the northbound bus no. 117.	*Se vuole arrivare a Palazzo Borghese, prenda il 117 in direzione Piazza Popolo/Villa Borghese.*
bus	l(o)'autobus/il bus
Bus no. 590 does Viale Trinità.	*Il 590 fa Viale Trinità.*
bus driver	il, la conducente
commute	fare il pendolare
commuter	il, la pendolare
course; route	il percorso
everywhere	dappertutto
exit; off	uscire; [l(a)'] uscita; [la] discesa; giù
ferryboat	il traghetto; il vaporetto
free	liberare; libero
get off	scendere
get on	salire
itinerary	il percorso
light railway	la metropolitana leggera
means of transportation	il mezzo di trasporto
meter	il tassametro
nowhere	da nessuna parte
out of service	fuori servizio
road	la strada
shuttle	la navetta
somewhere	da qualche parte
stop	fermare; fermarsi; la fermata
street	la via; la strada
Take the first street on your left after the traffic light.	*Prenda la prima via a sinistra dopo il semaforo.*

subway	la metropolitana/il, la metro, i metro
Kids enjoy riding the subway.	*Ai bambini piace prendere la metropolitana.*
taxi	[il, i] taxi/tassì
validate/stamp one's ticket	convalidare/obliterare il biglietto
way	il modo; la parte; la direzione
There are many ways to travel.	*Ci sono molti modi di viaggiare.*
The hospital is that way.	*L'ospedale è da quella parte/in quella direzione.*

Automobile | ## L'automobile

accident	l(o)'incidente
arrow	la freccia [direzionale]
battery	la batteria
beams	i fari
Did you turn on your high or low beams?	*Hai acceso i fari abbaglianti o gli anabbaglianti?*
brake	frenare; il freno
car	la macchina
drive	guidare
driver's license	la patente (di guida)
Did you go to driving school to get your driver's license?	*Sci andato a scuola guida per prendere la patente?*
economy car	l(a)'utilitaria
eighteen wheeler	il TIR; il camion a rimorchio

engine; motor	**il motore**
fill (the tank)	**fare il pieno**
flat tire	**la gomma a terra**
Oh, no, I got a flat tire again!	*Oh, no, ho una gomma a terra/ho bucato di nuovo!*
front	**anteriore**
gas station	**il distributore di benzina; il benzinaio** (m&f)
Does your car run on gasoline, methane, or diesel?	*La tua macchina va a benzina, a metano o a diesel?*
gear	**la marcia**
horn	**il clacson**
insurance policy	**la polizza d'assicurazione**
jack	**il cric**
license plates	**la targa [della macchina]**
rear	**posteriore**
rent a car	**noleggiare una macchina**
repair garage	**l(a)'officina [meccanica]; l'auto officina; il meccanico**
I have to take my car to the garage again.	*Devo portare di nuovo la macchina dal meccanico.*
reverse	**fare marcia indietro; la retromarcia**
ride	**cavalcare; viaggiare; il passaggio**
Do you want a ride?	*Vuoi un passaggio?*
run over	**investire**
shift	**cambiare; il cambio**
She never learned to shift gears well.	*Non ha mai imparato a cambiare bene le marce.*
tank	**il serbatoio**
truck	**il camion**
Truck drivers are a breed apart.	*I camionisti sono una razza speciale.*
valid [until]	**valido [fino a]**
wheel	**il volante** (steering); **la ruota** (tire)
windshield	**il parabrezza**
windshield wiper	**il tergicristallo**

Traffic

Il traffico/La circolazione [stradale]

above/over	[di] sopra
accelerate	accelerare
ahead; forward	avanti
avenue/boulevard	il corso/il viale
back	indietro
bridge	il ponte
The captain remained standing on the bridge while the ship was sinking.	*Il comandante restò immobile sul ponte mentre la nave affondava.*
cross	[at]traversare
curve	la curva
dead end	[il] vicolo cieco
detour	la deviazione
direction	l(a)'indicazione; la direzione
We're hopelessly lost; let's ask someone for directions.	*Ci siamo proprio persi; chiediamo indicazioni a qualcuno.*
If you keep going in that direction, you'll find the church.	*Se prosegue in quella direzione, troverà la chiesa.*
driveway	il passo carraio
fork (in road)	il bivio
forward	[in] avanti
get lost	perdersi
go back and forth	andare avanti e indietro
gridlock; traffic jam	l(o)'ingorgo
highway	l'autostrada [by definition, a toll road]
highway patrol	la polizia stradale
hitchhike	fare l(o)'autostop
impassable	intransitabile
lane	la corsia
That lane is only for public transport.	*Quella è la corsia preferenziale per i mezzi pubblici.*
map	la mappa; la cartina
one-way [street]	[strada a] senso unico

overpass	**il cavalcavia, i cavalcavia**
park (a car)	**parcheggiare**
parking meter	**il parchimetro**
pass	**[sor]passare; superare**
passerby	**il, la passante**
pedestrian	**il pedone** (m&f)
reach	**raggiungere; giungere a**
Did you reach your destination?	*Avete raggiunto la vostra meta?*
We reached our destination.	*Siamo giunti a destinazione.*
right-of-way	**il diritto di precedenza**
roadwork	**[i] lavori in corso**
road sign	**l(a)'indicazione/il segnale [stradale]**
I haven't seen a road sign in half an hour.	*Non vedo un'indicazione da mezz'ora.*
rush hour	**l'ora di punta**
school bus	**lo scuolabus, gli scuolabus**
slow down	**rallentare**
speed	**andare forte; la velocità**
speed limit	**il limite di velocità**
On Italian highways the speed limit is 130 kilometers per hour.	*Sulle autostrade italiane il limite di velocità è di 130 chilometri all'ora.*
stop [sign]	**lo stop**
straight ahead	**d[i]ritto**
ticket; fine	**la multa**
tollbooth	**il casello**
traffic light	**il semaforo**
Look at that traffic jam! All because the traffic light isn't working.	*Guarda che ingorgo! Tutto perché il semaforo è guasto.*
traffic policeman/woman	**il vigile [urbano]** (m&f)
tunnel	**il tunnel; la galleria**
turn	**girare; il giro**
You want to go straight for three blocks, then turn right on Via del Tritone.	*Vada diritto per tre isolati, poi giri a destra in Via del Tritone.*
two-way [street]	**[strada a] doppio senso**

under/below/beneath	[di] sotto
viaduct	il viadotto
yield	dare la precedenza

Vacations, Tourism, and Travel

## Vacations	## Le vacanze
cruise	la crociera
I like small cruise ships better.	*Preferisco le navi da crociera piccole.*
forest ranger	il, la guardaboschi, i guardaboschi; la guardia forestale (f&m)
go horseback riding	andare a cavallo
Do you want to go horseback riding with me on Saturday?	*Vuoi andare a cavallo con me sabato?*
have a long weekend/make a long weekend of it	fare il ponte
Thursday was a holiday and I took took Friday off, so I had a long weekend.	*Giovedì era festa e ho preso il venerdì di ferie, così ho fatto il ponte.*
natural park	il parco naturale
on foot	a piedi
outdoor	all(a)'aria aperta/all(o)'aperto
relax	rilassarsi; il relax
rest	riposarsi; il riposo
spend	passare (il tempo); spendere
stress	stressare; lo stress
For stress there is no better cure than two weeks at the beach.	*Per curare lo stress, non c'è niente di meglio di due settimane al mare.*
tired	stanco
vacation	la vacanza
weekend	il fine settimana/il weekend
We spent a beautiful weeklong vacation skiing in Colorado.	*Abbiamo passato una bellissima settimana bianca in Colorado.*

At the Beach

	In spiaggia
bathing suit	il costume da bagno
beach/deck chair	la sedia a sdraio
beachfront	il lungomare
beach resort	lo stabilimento balneare
beach toys	i giocattoli per la spiaggia
beach umbrella	l(o)'ombrellone
diver	il sub[acqueo], la sub[acquea]; i sub[acquei]
fins	le pinne
foosball	il calcetto/il calciobalilla
get a tan	abbronzarsi; prendere la tintarella
I got a great tan in Tahiti.	*Mi sono abbronzata proprio bene a Tahiti.*
go swimming	fare il bagno; andare a fare il bagno; nuotare; andare a nuotare
inflatable mattress	il materassino gonfiabile
lifeguard	il bagnino
oar	il remo
row	remare
sand	la sabbia
All children love building sand castles.	*A tutti i bambini piace costruire i castelli di sabbia.*
scuba diving	fare sub
sunblock	la crema antisolare
tan	l(a)'abbronzatura; la tintarella
waterskiing	lo sci d'acqua
waves	le onde; i cavalloni
I want to catch some more waves!	*Voglio giocare ancora un po' con i cavalloni!*
wet suit	la muta

Camping

	Il campeggio
camper	il campeggiatore
camper (van)	il camper

campfire	il fuoco
campground	il campeggio
flashlight	la pila; la torcia
freeze-dried rations	i pasti liofilizzati
mosquito repellent	l(a)'antizanzare
sleeping bag	il sacco a pelo
tent	la tenda
thermos	il termos
trailer	la roulotte

In the Mountains | ## In montagna

ascent	la salita
canteen	la borraccia
climb	arrampicare; fare alpinismo
She wants to do freestyle climbing.	*Vuole fare arrampicata libera.*
descent	la discesa
destination	la meta; la destinazione
face/wall (of rock)	la parete
[mountain] guide	la guida [alpina] (f&m)
hike	andare in gita; la gita/l(a)'escursione
We took a great hike in the lake region.	*Abbiamo fatto una bellissima escursione nella regione dei laghi.*
hiker	il, la gitante/l(o, a)'escursionista; gli escursionisti
ice ax	la picozza
mountain climber	l(o/a)'alpinista; gli alpinisti, le alpiniste
rope	la corda
rucksack	il sacco [da montagna]
shelter	il rifugio
slope	il pendio; la pista [da sci]
steep	ripido
summit; peak	la cima/la vetta
We reached the summit as the sun was rising.	*Siamo arrivati in vetta al sorgere del sole.*

trail	**il sentiero**
trekking	**il trekking**
walker	**[il] camminatore, [la] camminatrice**

Tourism   Il turismo

agricultural tourism	**l(o)'agriturismo**
My cousins are using their farmhouse as an inn for tourists who wish to spend their vacation on a farm.	*I miei cugini usano la loro casa colonica come pensione per i turisti che vogliono passare le vacanze in un agriturismo.*
antiquities	**le antichità**
archeological digs	**gli scavi archeologici**
castle	**il castello**
city of art	**la città d'arte**
exotic	**esotico**
go sightseeing	**fare del turismo**
[tourist] guide	**la guida [turistica]** (f&m)**; il cicerone**
holiday resort package	**il villaggio turistico**
package tour	**il viaggio organizzato**
panorama	**il panorama**
picturesque	**pittoresco**
stroll	**la passeggiata; il giro**
Come on, let's go for a stroll—it's such a nice day.	*Dài, andiamo a fare un giro—è una giornata magnifica.*
tour	**girare; il giro**
tourist information center	**[le] informazioni turistiche; l(o)'ufficio informazioni**
tour operator	**l(o)'operatore turistico**
typical	**tipico**

Travel   Viaggiare

arrival	**l(o)'arrivo**
arrive	**arrivare**
They arrived at their destination.	*Sono arrivati a destinazione.*

FF I finally understood what he meant.	*Ci sono arrivato, finalmente!*
cancel	**annullare/cancellare**
cancellation	**la cancellazione**
I cannot find any record of your cancellation, Sir.	*Non trovo nessun riscontro della sua cancellazione, Signore.*
catch/take	**prendere**
come	**venire**
confirm	**confermare**
confirmation	**la conferma**
connection	**la coincidenza**
I have a tight connection!	*Non no molto tempo per prendere la coincidenza!*
departure	**la partenza**
duffel bag	**la sacca**
fare	**la tariffa**
go	**andare**

 Must-Know Tip

Andare e venire translates as *coming and going* when used as a noun.

There was a lot of coming and going. **Era tutto un andare e venire.**

haste; hurry	**fare in fretta; la fretta** (sing. only)
Are you in such a hurry that you don't even have the time to say "Good morning"?	*Hai talmente tanta fretta che non hai tempo di dire 'Buon giorno'?*
hurry up	**sbrigarsi**
Let's hurry up, otherwise we'll miss the train!	*Sbrighiamoci, se no perdiamo il treno!*
journey/trip	**il viaggio**
leave	**partire**
We're leaving tomorrow.	*Partiamo domani.*
lost and found	**[gli] oggetti smarriti; [l(o)'] ufficio oggetti smarriti**

luggage storage/lockers	[il] deposito bagagli
medevac	l(a)'evacuazione medica
miss	perdere; mancare [a]
I missed the train.	*Ho perso il treno.*
Do you miss him a lot?	*Ti manca molto?*
one-way (ticket)	sola andata
I need a one-way ticket.	*Ho bisogno di un biglietto di sola andata.*
pack [one's suitcase]	fare la valigia
passenger	il passeggero
personal belongings	gli effetti personali
port of entry	lo scalo
put off; postpone	rimandare
refund	rimborsare; il rimborso
remain	rimanere/restare
reservation	la prenotazione
reserve	prenotare
restroom	la toilette
return	[ri]tornare; il ritorno
round-trip [ticket]	di andata e ritorno
schedule	l(o)'orario
seat	il posto; il sedile
Please make sure that your seat is in the upright position.	*Per favore, controllate che il vostro sedile sia in posizione verticale.*
This bus seats fifty people.	*Questo autobus ha posti a sedere per cinquanta persone.*
sit	sedersi
station	la stazione
take	volerci; metterci
It takes twelve hours to go from Turin to Rome, but I did it in eight.	*Ci vogliono dodici ore per andare da Torino a Roma, ma io ce ne ho messe solo otto.*
ticket	il biglietto
ticket counter	la biglietteria
travel agent	l(o, a)'agente di viaggio
travel warnings	gli avvisi per i viaggiatori

traveler	il viaggiatore, la viaggiatrice
tropical disease	la malattia tropicale
unpack	disfare le valigie
vaccination	la vaccinazione
visa	il visto
They entered the country with a tourist visa.	*Sono entrati nel paese con un visto turistico.*

Air Travel | ## Viaggiare in aereo

aboard; onboard	a bordo
Welcome aboard flight 45, with destination to Boston.	*Benvenuti a bordo del volo 45, con destinazione Boston.*
airline	la linea aerea
aircraft	l(o)'aeromobile
[air]plane	l(o)'aereo[plano]
airport	l(o)'aeroporto
airsickness	il mal d(i)'aria
aisle	(il) corridoio
altitude	l(a)'altitudine
baggage claim area	la zona/l(a)'area recupero bagagli/il ritiro bagagli
black box	la scatola nera
board	imbarcarsi
Ma'am, you can't board without a boarding pass.	*Signora, non può imbarcarsi senza la carta d'imbarco.*
boarding gate	la porta d'imbarco
captain	il comandante
carousel	il nastro trasportatore
carry-on [luggage]	il bagaglio a mano
cart	il carrello
check-in	la procedura d'imbarco/il check-in
I did an electronic check-in.	*Ho fatto il check-in elettronico.*
check luggage	imbarcare il bagaglio
class	la classe
Do you want to fly economy class or business class?	*Vuole volare in classe turistica o in classe business?*

control tower	**la torre di controllo**
crew	**l(o)'equipaggio**
customs	**[la] dogana**
Do you have anything to declare in customs?	*Ha qualcosa da dichiarare alla dogana?*
delay	**ritardare; il ritardo**
duty-free shop	**il duty free**
flight	**il volo**
Our flight was late.	*Il nostro volo era in ritardo.*
flight attendant	**l(o, a)'assistente di volo**
fly	**volare**
frequent flier program	**il programma di accumulo delle miglia**
ground transportation	**i trasporti a terra**
helicopter	**l(o)'elicottero**
jet	**il jet**
The Concorde was the only supersonic jet in commercial aviation.	*Il Concorde è stato l'unico jet supersonico dell'aviazione commerciale.*
jet lag	**il jet lag**
land	**atterrare; la terra**
The pilot had to land in the midst of a dangerous storm.	*Il pilota ha dovuto atterrare nel bel mezzo di un pericoloso temporale.*
landing	**l(o)'atterraggio**
metal detector	**il metal detector**
overbooking	**la sovraprenotazione/ l(o)'overbooking**
passport control	**[il] controllo passaporti**
pilot	**il, la pilota; i piloti**
radar	**il radar**
row	**[la] fila**
seat belt	**la cintura di sicurezza**
Please fasten your seat belts.	*Siete pregati di allacciare le cinture di sicurezza.*
security check	**il controllo sicurezza**
standby	**la riserva; lo standby**

take off; takeoff	**decollare; il decollo**
terminal	**il terminal**
tray table	**il tavolinetto**
window	**[il] finestrino**

Travel by Train

Viaggiare in treno

car (of a train)	**il vagone**
The restaurant car is after the sleeping car.	*Il vagone ristorante è dopo il vagone letto.*
cargo	**il carico; le merci**
compartment	**lo scompartimento**
conductor	**il bigliettaio; il capotreno**
container	**il container**
fast/quick; quickly	**veloce; velocemente**
The deer ran away so quickly that I barely got a glimpse of it.	*Il cervo è scappato così velocemente che ho fatto appena in tempo a vederlo.*
high-speed train	**il treno ad alta velocità (la TAV)**
locomotive	**la locomotiva**
platform	**la banchina**
railway/railroad	**la ferrovia**
railway station	**la stazione dei treni/ferroviaria**
slow	**lento; piano**
still/stopped	**fermo**
track	**il binario**

Travel by Ship

Viaggiare in nave

anchor	**gettare l'ancora; l(a)'ancora**
be shipwrecked	**naufragare**
cabin	**la cabina**
compass	**la bussola**
land	**sbarcare; la terra**
lifeboat	**la scialuppa di salvataggio**
lighthouse	**il faro**
marina	**il porticciolo; il porto turistico**

navigate	**navigare**
oil tanker	**la petroliera**
Oil rushed out of the tanker through a breach in the hold.	***Il petrolio fuoriuscì dalla petroliera attraverso una falla nella stiva.***
pier	**il molo; la banchina**
port	**il porto**
porthole	**l(o)'oblò**
seasickness	**il mal di mare**
siren	**la sirena**
tugboat	**il rimorchiatore**
wreck	**il relitto**

Eating Out / Mangiar fuori

bar	**il bar, i bar**
café	**il caffè, i caffè**
cafeteria	**la caffetteria**
chef	**lo chef** (m&f)
maitre d'	**il maitre** (m&f)
menu	**il menù**
neighborhood restaurant	**la trattoria**
pizzeria	**la pizzeria**
restaurant	**il ristorante**
seating	**il coperto**
self-service	**il self-service, i self-service**
sommelier	**il sommelier**
tip	**la mancia**
waiter/server	**il cameriere, la cameriera**
wine list	**la carta dei vini**

Accommodations and Hotels / Sistemazioni e alberghi

available	**disponibile**
bed and breakfast	**il bed and breakfast**
check in/check out	**prendere possesso della camera; lasciare la camera**
deposit	**il deposito**

disturb	**disturbare; il disturbo**
double room	**[la] camera doppia/matrimoniale**
extra	**gli extra**
front/reception desk	**la reception**
hotel chain	**la catena alberghiera**
hotel manager/owner	**l(a)'albergatore, l(a)'albergatrice**
included	**incluso**
inn/family-run hotel	**la pensione**
lobby; foyer	**la hall**
maid	**la cameriera** (a hotel maid, usually female)
pay the bill	**pagare/saldare il conto**
I'd like to pay the bill.	*Vorrei saldare il conto.*
receptionist	**il concierge**
room	**la camera**
room service	**il servizio in camera**
season	**la stagione**
In Florida winter is high season, and summer is low season.	*In Florida, la stagione invernale è alta stagione, quella estiva, bassa stagione.*
single room	**[la] camera singola**
time-sharing	**la comproprietà; il time-sharing**
vacancy	**[la] camera/stanza disponibile**
youth hostel	**l(o)'ostello della gioventù**

10

Government, Politics, and Society

Government and Politics

Nation, State, and the Nation-State

La nazione, lo stato e lo stato nazionale

belong	**appartenere**
boundary	**il confine**
citizen	**il cittadino**
citizenship	**la cittadinanza**
flag	**la bandiera**
frontier	**la frontiera**
identity	**l(a)'identità**
immigrant	**l(o, a)'immigrante**
immigration	**l(a)'immigrazione**
Clandestine immigration is one of the most serious issues in today's society.	*L'immigrazione clandestina è uno dei problemi più gravi della società contemporanea.*
inhabitant	**l(o, a)'abitante**
king	**il re, i re**
nationality	**la nazionalità**
patriot	**il, la patriota; i patrioti**
patriotism	**il patriottismo**
Patriotism in not a highly felt value in Italy.	*Il patriottismo non è un valore molto sentito in Italia.*
prince, princess	**il principe, la principessa**
queen	**la regina**
residency	**la residenza**
sovereignty	**la sovranità**
territory	**il territorio**

Government

Il governo

advisor	**il consigliere** (m&f)
against	**contro; contrario a**
assembly	**l(a)'assemblea**
authoritarian	**autoritario**
authorities	**le autorità**

They lived under an authoritarian regime, but not quite a dictatorial one. | *Sono vissuti in un regime autoritario, ma non proprio dittatoriale.*

be accountable [to] | **rispondere [delle proprie azioni] a**

He's been in power so long he feels he isn't accountable to anyone. | *È al potere da talmente tanto tempo che crede di non dover rispondere delle sue azioni a nessuno.*

branch | **il potere; il ramo; l'organo**

In modern democracy there are three separate branches of government: legislative, executive, and judiciary. | *Nella democrazia moderna ci sono tre poteri separati: il legislativo, l'esecutivo e il giudiziario.*

charismatic | **carismatico**

clarification | **il chiarimento**

confidence | **la fiducia**

The government asked Parliament for a vote of confidence. | *Il governo ha posto il voto di fiducia in Parlamento.*

consensus | **il consenso**

corruption | **la corruzione**

democracy | **la democrazia**

dictatorship | **la dittatura**

dissent | **dissentire; il dissenso**

domestic | **domestico; interno**

EU/European Union | **la EU/l(a)'Unione Europea**

European Commission | **la Commissione Europea**

filibuster/obstructionism | **l(o)'ostruzionismo**

government-/state-related | **statale**

in favor | **favorevole**

Some conservative representatives are in favor of a tough immigration law, but the majority is against. | *Alcuni parlamentari conservatori sono favorevoli ad una legge molto restrittiva sull'immigrazione, ma la maggioranza è contraria.*

institution | **l(a)'istituzione**

leader | **il, la leader; i, le leader(s)**

leadership | **la leadership**

The leadership of the party has been taken over by a new generation. | *La leadership del partito è passata a una nuova generazione.*

legitimacy	la legittimità
The Constitutional Court declared the law banning abortion illegitimate.	*La Corte Costituzionale ha dichiarato illegittima la legge che vietava l'aborto.*
monarchy	la monarchia
opposed	contrario
opposition	l(a)'opposizione
policy; politics	il provvedimento [politico]; la politica
City hall is working on a new policy to respond to the demands of young immigrants.	*Il consiglio municipale sta elaborando un nuovo provvedimento che risponda alle richieste dei giovani immigranti.*
She's always had a passion for politics.	*Ha sempre avuto una passione per la politica.*
political	politico; di parte
press conference	la conferenza stampa
public good	il bene comune
reform	riformare; la riforma
republic	la repubblica
scandal	lo scandalo
spokesperson	il, la portavoce
taxes	le tasse; le imposte
totalitarianism	il totalitarismo
welfare state	lo stato assistenziale; il welfare

Government Branches and Offices, Bureaucracy, and the Local Government

Gli organi e le cariche di governo, la burocrazia e il governo locale

administration	l(o)'amministrazione
bureau	l(o)'ufficio; l(o)'assessorato
certificate	il certificato
city hall	il municipio
civil servant	il funzionario (m&f), la funzionaria [dello stato/statale]

Council of Ministers	**il Consiglio dei Ministri**
delegate	**delegare; il delegato**
governor (of a region)	**il governatore**
mayor	**il sindaco** (m&f)
ministry of defense	**il ministero della difesa**
ministry of the economy	**il ministero dell(a)'economia**
ministry of foreign affairs	**il ministero degli esteri**
ministry of internal affairs	**il ministero dell'interno**
ministry of the treasury	**il ministero del tesoro**
Parliament	**il Parlamento**
president [of the republic]	**il presidente della repubblica**
prime minister	**il primo ministro** (m&f)**; il, la premier**
province	**la provincia**
We live in a large but provincial city.	*Viviamo in una città grande, ma provinciale.*
region	**la regione**
regulations	**il regolamento**
representative	**il deputato; il, la rappresentante**
senator	**il senatore, la senatrice**

Elections ## Le elezioni

ballot	**la scheda**
A blank ballot is a form of abstention, while voiding out one's ballot is a way of expressing one's dissent.	*Votare scheda bianca è una forma di astensione, mentre annullare la scheda è un modo per esprimere il proprio dissenso.*
campaign	**la campagna**
candidate	**il candidato**
Is it really true that your mother has decided to run for the Senate?	*È proprio vero che tua madre ha deciso di presentarsi candidata al Senato?*
concede	**concedere**
debate	**dibattere; il dibattito**
elect	**eleggere**

electoral fraud	il broglio elettorale
exit polls	i sondaggi postelettorali/gli exit poll[s]
majority	la maggioranza
participation	la partecipazione
polling station	il seggio [elettorale]
primaries	le primarie
referendum	il referendum
seat	il seggio [in parlamento]
vote	votare; il voto
voter	l(o)'elettore; l(a)'elettrice

Major Political Parties / I maggiori partiti politici

Christian Democratic Center	[il] Centro Cristiano Democratico (CCD)
Christian Democratic Union	[l(a)']Unione Democratici Cristiani (UDC)
Communist Renewal	Rifondazione Comunista (RC)
Daisy	La Margherita
Democrats of the Left	[i] Democratici della Sinistra (DS)
Go Italy	Forza Italia
Greens	[la] Federazione dei Verdi
National Alliance	Alleanza Nazionale (AN)
Northern League	La Lega Nord
Olive Tree	l(o)'Ulivo

Ideologies / Le ideologie

anarchic	[l(o)'] anarchico
anarchy	l(a)'anarchia

 Must-Know Tip

Italians are so attached to their own towns that the ideology expressing that attitude is called **campanilismo**, from **campanile**.

center	**il centro**
communism	**il comunismo**
conservatives	**i conservatori**
equality	**l(a)'uguaglianza**
fairness	**la giustizia; l(a)'equità**
fascism	**il fascismo**
freedom/liberty	**la libertà**
fundamentalism	**il fondamentalismo**
left	**[la] sinistra**
liberalism	**il liberalismo; il movimento progressista**

Liberalism began in the nineteenth century as an ideology in favor of the free market. — *Il liberalismo emerse nel diciannovesimo secolo come un'ideologia a sostegno del libero mercato.*

moderates	**i moderati**
nazism	**il nazismo**
populism	**il populismo**
public opinion	**l(a)'opinione pubblica**
radical	**[il] radicale**
rank and file	**la base [del partito]**
regime	**il regime**
resistance	**la resistenza**
revolution	**[la] rivoluzione**
right	**[la] destra**
social democracy	**la socialdemocrazia**
socialism	**il socialismo**

Civil Society — La società civile

abortion rights movement	**il movimento per il diritto all(o)'aborto**
antiglobalization movement	**il movimento antiglobalizzazione/antiglobal**
aristocracy	**l(a)'aristocrazia**

bourgeois	[il, la] borghese
Central Italy	il Centro
North, Center, and South refer not only to geographic areas of Italy, but also to different socioeconomic and anthropologic areas.	*Il Nord, il Centro e il Sud non identificano solo delle zone geografiche dell'Italia, ma anche delle diverse realtà socioeconomiche e antropologiche.*
class	la classe [sociale]
The middle and working classes are more and more similar from a socioeconomic point of view.	*La classe media e la classe operaia sono sempre più simili dal punto di vista socioeconomica.*
community	la comunità
demonstration	la dimostrazione
discriminate	discriminare
discrimination	la discriminazione
Racial, sexual, and religious discrimination has become an important issue in the last thirty years.	*La discriminazione razziale, sessuale e religiosa è diventata un problema importante negli ultimi trent'anni.*
diversity	la diversità
elite	l(a)'élite, le élite
ethnic minority	la minoranza etnica
feminism	il femminismo
feminist	[la] femminista (rarely used in masc.)
gay rights movement	il movimento per i diritti degli omosessuali
homeless person	il, la i senzatetto
The city opened a homeless shelter in our neighborhood.	*Il comune ha aperto un centro di accoglienza per i senzatetto nel nostro quartiere.*
intolerance	l(a)'intolleranza
masses	le masse
multiculturalism	il multiculturalismo
privacy	la privacy

progress	progredire; il progresso
pro-life	per la vita; antiabortista
prostitute	la prostituta
prostitution	la prostituzione
protest	protestare; la protesta
race	la razza
racism	il razzismo
Racism is rising in Italy together with the increasing number of immigrants from non-EU countries.	*Il razzismo è in aumento in Italia con l'aumento dell'immigrazione dai paesi extracomunitari.*
secular	laico
solidarity	la solidarietà
tolerance	la tolleranza
FF You're too indulgent with our children.	*Tu sei troppo tollerante coi bambini.*
tradition	la tradizione
transgender	il, la transessuale
transvestite	il travestito (masc. only)
value	apprezzare; valutare; il valore
volunteer	il volontario

Law and Order

Judiciary — La magistratura

claim	esigere; il diritto
constitution	la costituzione
Constitutional Court	la Corte Costituzionale
court	il tribunale
duty	il dovere
interrogatory	l(o)'interrogatorio
judge	giudicare; il giudice (m&f)
juror	il giurato
jury	la giuria
justice	la giustizia

juvenile court	**il tribunale dei minori**
law; right	**la legge; il diritto**

Must-Know Tip

English does not have an equivalent of Italian **diritto,** which means both *right* (and in the plural, **diritti,** *rights*), and the set of rights and duties that comprise a legal system.

lawsuit	**la causa**
notary public	**il notaio** (m&f)

Must-Know Tip

An Italian **notaio** performs much more important functions than a notary public in the United States. The **notaio** is a highly paid lawyer who manages all the procedural aspects of contracts and documents.

record	**mettere a verbale; il verbale**
Her testimony has been put on the record.	*La sua testimonianza è stata messa a verbale.*
rule	**governare; la regola**
He ruled the country for forty years.	*Ha governato il paese per quarant'anni.*
sue	**fare causa**
trial	**il processo**
try	**processare**
He was tried for drug trafficking.	*È stato processato per traffico di stupefacenti.*

Law and Order   La legge e l(o)'ordine

acquit	**assolvere**
arrest	**arrestare; l(o)'arresto**
bail	**la cauzione**

Carabinieri Corps	l'Arma dei Carabinieri
case	il caso
FF They met by chance.	*Si sono conosciuti per caso.*
cell	la cella
charge	accusare; il capo d'accusa
checkpoint; road block	il posto di blocco
confess	confessare
criminal	[il, la] criminale; [il, la] delinquente
custody	la custodia
death penalty	la pena di morte
defendant	l(o)'imputato
defense	la difesa
[police] detective	il commissario (m&f); l(o)'ispettore, l(a)'ispettrice [di polizia]
district attorney	il PM (Pubblico Ministero) (m&f), la PM
electric chair	la sedia elettrica
enforce	far rispettare le leggi
evidence; proof	l(a)'evidenza; la prova
You can't deny the evidence.	*Non puoi negare l'evidenza.*
execution	l(a)'esecuzione
executioner	il carnefice
frisk	perquisire
guilt	la colpa; la colpevolezza
It's all your fault!	*È tutta colpa tua!*
guilty	[il] colpevole
He has been found guilty of embezzlement.	*È stato dichiarato colpevole di appropriazione indebita.*
handcuffs	le manette
hang	impiccare
informer	l(o)'informatore (l'informatrice, rare)
innocent	[l(o, a)'] innocente
investigation	l(a)'inchiesta; l(a)'investigazione
jail; prison	la prigione; il carcere

lawyer	l(o)'avvocato (m&f) (l[a]'avvocatessa, rare)
lie	mentire; la menzogna; dire le bugie; la bugia
life sentence	l(o)'ergastolo; la condanna a vita
He got a life sentence.	*Gli hanno dato l(o)'ergastolo.*
oath	il giuramento
plaintiff	il, la querelante
plead	dichiararsi
police	la polizia
policeman/police officer	il poliziotto (m&f); la poliziotta (rare)
prisoner	il detenuto; il prigioniero
private detective	l(o)'investigatore privato; l(a)'investigatrice privata
probation	la libertà vigilata
release	rilasciare
suspect	sospettare; il sospetto; sospetto
suspicious	sospettoso
testimony	la testimonianza
Her testimony has been crucial at the trial against the mafia boss.	*La sua testimonianza è stata di importanza cruciale al processo contro il boss mafioso.*
witness	il, la testimone

Crimes and Felonies / Delitti e reati

abuse	l(o)'abuso
accomplice	il, la complice
blackmail	ricattare; il ricatto
blackmailer	il ricattatore, la ricattatrice
bribe; kickback	corrompere; la tangente; la bustarella
child abduction	la sottrazione di minore
counterfeiter	il falsario
escape	evadere; l(a)'evasione
harm	danneggiare; il danno

harass	**molestare**
harassment	**la molestia**
I filed a grievance against my boss for sexual harassment.	*Ho inoltrato un ricorso contro il mio capo per molestia sessuale.*
identity theft	**il furto di identità**
kidnap	**rapire; sequestrare**
money laundering	**il riciclaggio di denaro sporco**
organized crime	**il crimine organizzato**
piracy	**la pirateria**
rape	**stuprare; lo stupro**
rob	**rapinare; derubare**
They robbed our neighborhood's bank for the third time.	*Hanno rapinato la banca nel nostro quartiere per la terza volta.*
Stop him! He just robbed me!	*Fermatelo! Mi ha derubato!*
robber	**il rapinatore, la rapinatrice; i rapinatori, le rapinatrici**
Armed robbery is a serious crime.	*La rapina a mano armata è un reato serio.*
self-defense	**l(a)'autodifesa/la legittima difesa**
slander	**calunniare; la calunnia; diffamare; la diffamazione**
smuggling	**il contrabbando**
steal	**rubare**
They stole two paintings by Chagall.	*Hanno rubato due quadri di Chagall.*
He stole my briefcase from me!	*Mi ha rubato la cartella!*
thief	**il ladro**
trafficking	**il traffico**
victim	**la vittima**

International Politics

International Relations and Diplomacy

Le relazioni internazionali e la diplomazia

abroad; overseas	**all(o)'estero**
ally	**l(o)'alleato**

ambassador	l(o)'ambasciatore (m&f)/ l(a)'ambasciatrice
colonialism	il colonialismo
consul	il console (m&f)
consulate	il consolato
cooperation	la cooperazione
democratization	la democratizzazione
deterrence	la deterrenza
dialogue	il dialogo
disarmament	il disarmo
embassy	l(a)'ambasciata
empire	l(o)'impero
imperialism	l(o)'imperialismo
liberation	la liberazione
mediator	il mediatore, la mediatrice
power	il potere; la potenza
The United States is now the only superpower.	*Adesso gli Stati Uniti sono l'unica superpotenza.*
resolution	la risoluzione
sanctions	le sanzioni
security	la sicurezza
summit	il vertice
third world	il terzo mondo
treaty	il trattato
U.N./United Nations Organization	l(a)'ONU/l(a)'Organizzazione delle Nazioni Unite
unanimity	l(a)'unanimità
unite	unire
veto	porre il veto; il veto

War and Peace

Guerra e pace

alert	l(a)'allerta; l(o)'avviso
attack	attaccare; l(o)'attacco
battle	la battaglia
casualties	i caduti

cease-fire	**il cessate il fuoco**
challenge	**sfidare; la sfida**
code	**il codice**
cold war	**la guerra fredda**
confrontation	**il confronto**
conquer	**conquistare**
conquest	**la conquista**
coup d'état	**il colpo di stato; il golpe**
courage	**il coraggio**
cowardice	**la viltà**
cryptography	**la crittografia**
danger/hazard	**il pericolo**
defeat	**sconfiggere; la sconfitta**
desert	**disertare**
destroy	**distruggere**
discipline	**la disciplina**
duel	**duellare/il duello**
enemy/foe	**il nemico**
enemy combatant	**il nemico combattente**
escalation	**l(a)'escalation**
fight/combat	**combattere; il combattimento**
front	**il fronte**
All quiet on the western front.	*Niente di nuovo sul fronte occidentale.*
guerrilla	**la guerriglia**
hero	**l(o)'eroe, l(a)'eroina**
incident	**l(o)'incidente**
The incident that involved the two submarines brought us to the brink of war.	*L'incidente che coinvolse i due sottomarini ci portò sull'orlo della guerra.*
independence	**l(a)'indipendenza**
intelligence	**le informazioni; l(a)'intelligence**
A spy who infiltrated the intelligence agency gave the enemy access to top-secret documents.	*Una spia che si è infiltrata nel servizio di informazioni ha fatto pervenire al nemico dei documenti riservati.*

invasion	l(a)'invasione
kill	uccidere; l(a)'uccisione
make peace	fare la pace
neutrality	la neutralità
peacekeeping mission	la missione di pace
secret	[il] segreto
spy	spiare; la spia
strategy	la strategia
surrender	arrendersi; la resa
At the end of World War II, Japan surrendered unconditionally.	*Alla fine della Seconda guerra mondiale la resa del Giappone fu incondizionata.*
tactic	la tattica
truce	la tregua
ultimatum	l(o)'ultimatum
violence	la violenza
wound	ferire; la ferita

Military — Le forze armate

academy	l(a)'accademia
admiral	l(o)'ammiraglio (m&f)
air force	l(a)'aeronautica [militare]; l(a)'aviazione
army	l(o)'esercito
command center	il comando
conscientious objector	l(o)'obiettore di coscienza
court martial	la corte marziale
draft	la leva
general	[il] generale (m&f)
navy	la marina [militare]
officer	l(o)'ufficiale (m&f)
soldier	il soldato (m&f)
rations	le razioni
troops	le truppe

Armaments and Weapons

aircraft carrier	**la portaerei, le portaerei**
air raid	**il bombardamento [aereo]**
bomb	**bombardare; la bomba**
bomber	**il cacciabombardiere**
fleet	**la flotta**
grenade	**la granata**
machine gun	**la mitragliatrice**
missile	**il missile**
The missile carried five nuclear warheads.	*Il missile era dotato di cinque testate nucleari.*
pistol/gun	**la pistola**
rank	**il grado**
rocket	**il razzo**
satellite	**il satellite**
submarine	**il sottomarino**
tank	**il carro armato**
weapons of mass destruction	**le armi di distruzione di massa**
Atomic, biological, and chemical weapons are weapons of mass destruction.	*Le armi atomiche, biologiche e chimiche sono armi di distruzione di massa.*

Human Rights

aid	**aiutare; l(o)'aiuto**
airlift	**il ponte aereo**
asylum	**l(o)'asilo [politico]**
civil disobedience	**la disobbedienza civile**
donations	**le donazioni**
emergency	**l(a)'emergenza**
evacuation	**l(a)'evacuazione**
famine	**la carestia**
human being	**l(o)'essere umano, gli esseri umani**
humanity	**l(a)'umanità**
Humanity has engaged in warfare throughout its history.	*L'umanità ha sempre fatto la guerra.*

intervention	l(o)'intervento
The role of NGOs (nongovernmental organizations) in humanitarian intervention is growing.	*Il ruolo delle ONG (organizzazioni non governative) negli interventi umanitari è in aumento.*
men	gli uomini
Human beings are strange animals.	*Gli uomini sono strani animali.*
pacifism	il pacifismo
reconstruction	la ricostruzione
refugee	il rifugiato; lo sfollato
relief	il soccorso
respect	rispettare; il rispetto
protect	proteggere
slave	lo schiavo
slavery	la schiavitù
starve	soffrire la fame
survive	sopravvivere
torture	torturare; la tortura
violation	la violazione

Terrorism and Nonconventional Warfare
Il terrorismo e la guerra nonconvenzionale

ambush	tendere un(a)'imboscata; l(a)'imboscata
attempt (against someone's life)	l(o)'attentato
betray	tradire
blast	esplodere; l(a)'esplosione
capture	catturare; la cattura
car bomb	la macchina bomba
civilians	i civili
crusade	la crociata
ethnic cleansing	la pulizia etnica
faction	la fazione
force	costringere/forzare; la forza
genocide	il genocidio
go underground	darsi alla macchia
hate	odiare; l(o)'odio

hide	**nascondere**
hijack	**dirottare**
hijacker	**il dirottatore, la dirottatrice**
The hijackers held the passengers and the crew hostage.	*I dirottatori presero in ostaggio l'equipaggio e i passeggeri.*
holocaust	**l(o)'olocausto**
insurgents	**gli insorti**
mob; crowd	**la folla**
revenge	**la vendetta**
sabotage	**sabotare; il sabotaggio**
sympathizer	**il, la simpatizzante**
terrorist	**[il, la] terrorista**
threat	**minacciare; la minaccia**
traitor	**il traditore, la traditrice; i traditori, le traditrici**

11

Earth, Nature, and the Environment

Space and Earth

Space

astronomy

black hole

chaos

comet

constellation

dimension

expand

finite

We don't know whether the universe is finite or infinite.

flying saucer

galaxy

gravity

light

It is maintained that it will never be possible to travel at the speed of light.

mass

matter

meteorite

Milky Way

nebula

observatory

orbit

shooting star

spectrum

FF Have you seen a ghost?

star

The North Star and the Southern Cross help navigators to orient themselves.

telescope

Lo spazio

l(a)'astronomia

il buco nero

il caos

la cometa

la costellazione

la dimensione

espandersi

finito

Non si sa se l'universo sia finito o infinito.

il disco volante

la galassia

la gravità

la luce

Si ritiene che non sarà mai possibile viaggiare alla velocità della luce.

la massa

la materia

il meteorite

la Via Lattea

la nebulosa

l(o)'osservatorio

orbitare; l(a)'orbita

la stella cadente

lo spettro

Hai visto uno spettro?/un fantasma?

la stella

La Stella Polare e la Croce del Sud aiutano i naviganti a orientarsi.

il telescopio; il cannocchiale

universe	l'universo
vacuum	il vuoto
zodiac	lo zodiaco

Solar System | ## Il sistema solare

| asteroid | l(o)'asteroide |
| eclipse | l(a)'eclissi |

There will be a partial solar eclipse and a total lunar eclipse two weeks from one another. | *Ci sarà un'eclissi parziale di sole ed una totale di luna a due settimane di distanza l'una dall'altra.*

focus	il fuoco
Jupiter	Giove
Mars	Marte
Mercury	Mercurio
moon	la luna
Neptune	Nettuno
planet	il pianeta, i pianeti
Pluto	Plutone
ray	il raggio
rotation	la rotazione
Saturn	Saturno
sun	il sole
Uranus	Urano
Venus	Venere

Earth | ## La Terra

air	l(a)'aria
arctic/antarctic circle	il circolo polare artico/antartico
atmosphere	l(a)'atmosfera
core	il centro [della Terra]
east	[l(o)'] est/[l(o)'] oriente
equator	l(o)'equatore
globe	il globo
hemisphere	l(o)'emisfero
latitude	la latitudine

longitude	la longitudine
The coordinates of Rome are:	*Le coordinate di Roma sono:*
41°54′ N latitude —	*41°54′ latitudine nord e 12°29′*
12°29′ E longitude.	*longitudine est.*
magma	il magma
meridian	il meridiano
north	[il] nord/il settentrione
oxygen	l(o)'ossigeno
parallel	il parallelo
polar ice cap	la calotta polare
The polar ice cap is melting.	*La calotta polare si sta sciogliendo.*
pole	il polo
south	[il] sud/il meridione
sky	il cielo
stratosphere	la stratosfera
Tropic of Cancer/Capricorn	il Tropico del Cancro/del Capricorno
west	[l(o)'] ovest/[l(o)'] occidente
zenith	lo zenit

Land

Le terre emerse

archipelago	l(o)'arcipelago
cave	la grotta; la caverna
cliff	la scogliera
coastline	la costa
continent	il continente
edge	l(o)'orlo; il bordo
ground	il suolo
There's a lot of water deep below ground.	*C'è molta acqua nel sottosuolo.*
hill	la collina
island	l(a)'isola
meadow	il prato
mountain chain/ridge	la catena montuosa
pass	il passo; il colle

peninsula	**la penisola**
plain	**la pianura**
plateau	**l'altipiano**
rock	**la roccia**
valley	**la valle**

Water — ## Le acque

bank	**la riva**
bay	**la baia**
bottom	**il fondo; il fondale**
calm	**calmo**
canal; channel	**il canale**
The tunnel under the English Channel is called the Chunnel.	*Il tunnel sotto il Canale della Manica viene chiamato il 'Chunnel'.*
Do you know how many canals there are in Venice?	*Sai quanti sono i canali di Venezia?*
cape	**[il] capo**
deep	**profondo**
dune	**la duna**
flow; current	**scorrere; la corrente; sfociare**
The Tiber River flows into the Tyrrhenian Sea.	*Il Tevere sfocia nel Mar Tirreno.*
glacier	**il ghiacciaio**
gulf	**il golfo**
If water melting from the polar ice cap cools the Gulf Stream, European countries will become much colder.	*Se la calotta polare si scioglie, l'acqua raffredderà la Corrente del Golfo e i paesi europei diventeranno molto più freddi.*
high/tall	**alto**
high sea	**[l(o)'] alto mare**
iceberg	**l(o)'iceberg**
lagoon	**la laguna**
lake	**il lago**
low	**basso**
marsh	**la palude**

mouth (of river)	**la foce**
mud	**il fango**
I have a terrible backache. I should go to a spa for mud therapy.	***Ho un mal di schiena terribile, dovrei andare a fare i fanghi.***
ocean	**l(o)'oceano**
He has crossed the Atlantic, Indian, and Pacific oceans with his catamaran.	***Ha attraversato l'oceano Indiano, l'Atlantico e il Pacifico in catamarano.***
quicksand	**le sabbie mobili**
river	**il fiume**
That river has thirteen tributaries.	***Qual fiume ha tredici immissari.***
sea	**il mare**
shallow	**basso; poco profondo**
shore/shoreline	**la riva; la costa**
source/spring	**la sorgente (del fiume); la fonte; la sorgente**
The water from that spring is delicious.	***L'acqua di quella sorgente è deliziosa.***
strait	**lo stretto**
stream	**il ruscello; il torrente**
tide	**la marea**
The tide ebbs and flows every six hours.	***La marea sale e scende ogni sei ore.***
water	**l(a)'acqua**
Human beings can only drink freshwater, not saltwater.	***Gli esseri umani possono bere solo l'acqua dolce, non quella salata.***
waterfall	**la cascata**

Weather and Seasons

Seasons and Climates	**Le stagioni e i climi**
cold	**freddo**
dry	**secco**
equinox	**l(o)'equinozio**
fall/autumn	**l(o)'autunno**
polar	**polare**

solstice	**il solstizio**
spring	**la primavera**
summer	**l(a)'estate**
temperate	**temperato**
tropical	**tropicale**
wet	**bagnato**
Our dog got completely wet.	*Il cane si è bagnato tutto.*
winter	**l(o)'inverno**

Weather Conditions — Le condizioni del tempo

clear [up]	**aprirsi; rasserenarsi; schiarire**
climate	**il clima**
cloud	**la nuvola**
cloudy	**nuvoloso**
It's been cloudy for a month.	*È nuvoloso così da un mese.*
cool	**fresco**
fog	**la nebbia**
freeze	**gelare; il gelo/la gelata**
hail	**grandinare; la grandine**
haze	**l(a)'afa**
hot	**molto caldo**

 Must-Know Tip

[Il tempo] è caldo, translates to: *It's cold.* **[La giornata] è fredda**, translates to: *It's a cold day.* But we mostly use the construction: **fare caldo, freddo, brutto, bello, ecc.** (only in the third person singular, followed by an adjective in the masculine).

It's cold.	*Fa caldo.*
It's warm.	*Fa freddo.*

ice	**il ghiaccio**
lightning	**il fulmine**
overcast	**coperto; nuvoloso**
rain	**piovere; la pioggia**

Must-Know Tip

Verbs expressing weather conditions are impersonal in Italian, are conjugated in the third-person singular, can take **essere** or **avere** as their auxiliaries in compound tenses, and *don't* carry any subject.

It's snowing.	**Sta nevicando.**
It's thundering, but it's not raining.	**Tuona, ma non piove.**
It snowed.	**È/Ha nevicato.**

rainbow	l(o)'arcobaleno
shade/shadow	l(o)'ombra
Do you want to sit in the sun or in the shade?	*Vuoi sederti al sole o all'ombra?*
The mountain cast a long shadow onto the valley.	*La montagna proiettava una lunga ombra sulla vallata.*
snow	nevicare; la neve
snowflake	il fiocco di neve
storm	il temporale; la tempesta
sweltering; torrid	torrido
thaw	sciogliere; sciogliersi; il disgelo
thunder	tuonare; il tuono
warm	caldo
wind	il vento

Extreme Weather Conditions and Natural Disasters
Condizioni climatiche estreme e disastri naturali

ash	la cenere
avalanche	la valanga/la slavina
catastrophe	la catastrofe
crater	il cratere
cyclone	il ciclone
dam/dike	la diga
drought	la siccità
earthquake	il terremoto
flood	inondare; l(a)'inondazione

hurricane	l(o)'uragano
landslide	la frana
lava	la lava
shake	scuotere; la scossa
smoke	il fumo
snowstorm	la tormenta
tornado; whirlwind	il tornado; la tromba d'aria
tsunami	il maremoto; lo tsunami
typhoon	il tifone
volcano	il vulcano
wildfire	l(o)'incendio

Weather Forecast

Le previsioni del tempo

average	[la] media
barometer	il barometro
degree	il grado
maximum	[la] massima
meteorologist	il meteorologo
meteorology	la meteorologia
minimum	[la] minima
pressure	la pressione
A high-pressure zone will replace the low-pressure zone that has given us such bad weather.	*Un'area di alta pressione sostituirà l'area di bassa pressione che ci ha portato tanto maltempo.*
report/bulletin	il bollettino
take shelter	ripararsi; cercare rifugio
temperature	la temperatura
variable	variabile
warning	l(o)'avviso

Ecology

L(a)'ecologia

biomass	la biomassa
blackout	il blackout
conservation	la conservazione
electric; electrical	elettrico

endangered species	la specie [le specie] in via di estinzione
energy	l(a)'energia
There are many sources of alternative energy.	*Esistono molte fonti di energia alternativa.*
environment	l(o)'ambiente
environmentalist	l(o, a)'ambientalista
erosion	l(a)'erosione
geology	la geologia
nature	la natura
recycle	riciclare
renewable	rinnovabile
reuse	riutilizzare; il riutilizzo
solar panels	i pannelli solari
sustainable	sostenibile

Pollution   L(o)'inquinamento

acid	acido
carbon dioxide	l(a)'anidride carbonica
coal	il carbone
contamination	la contaminazione
decibel	i decibel
deforestation	il disboscamento
desertification	la desertificazione
endangered species	la specie in via di estinzione
fuel	rifornire di carburante; il carburante
garbage dumpster	il cassonetto dei rifiuti
gasoline; gas	le benzina; il gas
global warming	il riscaldamento globale
greenhouse effect	l(o)'effetto serra
hydrocarbons	gli idrocarburi
impact	avere un impatto; l(o)'impatto
incinerator	l(o)'inceneritore
lead	il piombo
nitrogen	l(o)'azoto

noise	il rumore
oil	il petrolio
ozone layer	lo strato dell(o)'ozono
particle	la particella
passive smoking	il fumo passivo
pesticide	il pesticida, i pesticidi
plant	piantare; la pianta; la centrale; l'impianto

He has one hundred fifty species of plants in his garden.

Ha centocinquanta specie di piante nel giardino.

They dismantled the hydroelectric plant to save the salmon.

Hanno smantellato la centrale idroelettrica per salvare i salmoni.

reforestation	il rimboschimento
risk assessment	la valutazione del rischio
smog	lo smog
throw away/out	gettare/buttare [via]
waste	sprecare; lo spreco
windmill	il mulino a vento

Farming and Gardening

Agriculture and Zootechnics   L(a)'agricoltura e la zootecnia

barley	l(o)'orzo
barn	il fienile; il granaio
breed/rear	allevare
chicken coop	il pollaio
corn	il granoturco/il mais
corral; pen	il recinto
cultivate	coltivare
farm	la fattoria/l'azienda agricola
farmer	l'agricoltore (m&f)
feed	nutrire
field	il campo
genetically modified organisms (GMO)	gli organismi geneticamente modificati (OGM)

harvest	il raccolto; mietere; la mietitura; vendemmiare; la vendemmia
hay	il fieno
in season	di stagione
irrigation	l(a)'irrigazione
milk	mungere; il latte
organic	biologico; organico
My uncle has been doing organic agriculture for twenty years.	*Mio zio fa agricoltura biologica da vent'anni.*
peasant	il contadino
rancher	l(o)'allevatore; l(a)'allevatrice (di bestiame)
His grandparents are cattle ranchers, but they also rear poultry.	*I suoi nonni sono allevatori di bestiame, ma allevano anche il pollame.*
rice field	la risaia
rye	la segale
soil	il terreno
stable	la stalla
till	dissodare
vineyard	la vigna/il vigneto
wheat	il grano
winegrower	il viticoltore

Farming and Gardening Tools / Gli attrezzi per l'agricoltura e il giardinaggio

barrel	la botte; il barile
fertilizer	il fertilizzante
gardener	il giardiniere, la giardiniera (rare)
hoe	la zappa
[watering] hose	il tubo [per innaffiare]
manure	il concime
nursery	il vivaio
pitchfork	il tridente; il forcone
plough	arare; l(o)'aratro
prune	potare

rake	rastrellare; il rastrello
saw	segare; la sega
seed	seminare; il seme
shears	le cesoie
shovel	spalare; la pala
spade	la vanga
tractor	il trattore
vegetable garden	l(o)'orto
water	bagnare (i fiori, i campi); annaffiare/innaffiare
watering can	l(o)'annaffiatoio/l(o)'innaffiatoio
wheelbarrow	la carriola

Trees — Gli alberi

acacia	l(a)'acacia
beech	il faggio
birch	la betulla
cactus	il cactus
chestnut	il castagno
deciduous	caduco/deciduo
eucalyptus	l(o)'eucalipto
evergreen	[il] sempreverde
fell	abbattere
fir	l(o)'abete
flora	la flora
forest	la foresta
grass	l(a)'erba
leaf	la foglia
maple	l(o)'acero
oak	la quercia
oleander	l(o)'oleandro
palm	la palma
pine	il pino

The Mediterranean pine tree is shaped like an umbrella and produces big cones.

Il pino mediterraneo ha una forma ad ombrello e produce delle grosse pigne.

poplar	**il pioppo**
root	**la radice**
walnut	**il noce**
willow	**il salice**
wood	**il bosco; la legna** (for burning); **il legno** (as material)

The little girl got lost in the woods. *La ragazzina si smarrì nel bosco.*
Did you cut enough firewood *Hai tagliato abbastanza legna per*
for winter? *l'inverno?*

Flowers and Shrubs / I fiori e i cespugli

carnation	**il garofano**
clematis	**la clematide**
daffodil	**il tromboncino; la giunchiglia**
daisy	**la margherita**
hydrangea	**l(o)'ortensia**
iris	**l(o)'iris**
ivy	**l(a)'edera**
lavender	**la lavanda**
lily	**il giglio**
moss	**il muschio**
narcissus	**il narciso**
orchid	**l(a)'orchidea**
pansy	**la viola del pensiero**
petunia	**la petunia**
tulip	**il tulipano**
violet	**la violetta**

Animals

Pets / Gli animali di casa

blackbird	**il merlo**
canary	**il canarino**
cat	**il gatto**
dog	**il cane; la cagnetta**
goldfish	**il pesce rosso**

hamster	il criceto
muzzle	il muso
parrot	il pappagallo
paw	la zampa
peacock	il pavone
pony	il pony
tail	la coda
turtle/tortoise	la tartaruga

Domestic Animals / Gli animali domestici

bull	il toro
camel	il cammello
cow	la mucca/la vacca
cry/call (of an animal)	il verso
donkey	l(o)'asino
flock	il gregge
goat	la capra
goose	l(o)'oca
hen	la gallina
The hen hatched ten chicks.	*La gallina ha covato dieci pulcini.*
herd	la mandria
llama	il lama, i lama
ox	il bue, i buoi
pig	il maiale
rooster	il gallo
The rooster crows for the first time at 3 A.M.	*Il gallo canta per la prima volta alle tre.*
sheep	la pecora
tame	domare/addomesticare
veterinarian	il veterinario

Wild Animals / Gli animali selvatici

alligator	l(o)'alligatore
antelope	l(a)'antilope
bear	l(o)'orso
buffalo	il bufalo; il bisonte

coyote	**il coyote, i coyote**
crocodile	**il coccodrillo**
deer	**il cervo**
elephant	**l(o)'elefante**

 Must-Know Tip

Some names of animals are masculine and others are feminine, independently of the gender of the individual animal in question: **l(o)'elefante** is masculine; **la tigre** is feminine. Domestic animals often have both masculine and feminine versions: **il cavallo** (horse), **la cavalla** (mare); **il gallo** (rooster), **la gallina** (hen); **il gatto** (he-cat), **la gatta** (she-cat), etc.

fangs	**le zanne**
fauna	**la fauna**
fox	**la volpe**
gazelle	**la gazzella**
giraffe	**la giraffa**
hedgehog	**il riccio**
hide	**la pelle (di un animale)**
hippopotamus	**l(o)'ippopotamo**
hyena	**la iena**
ibex	**lo stambecco**
jackal	**lo sciacallo**
jaguar	**il giaguaro**
kangaroo	**il canguro**
leopard	**il leopardo**
lion	**il leone**
lioness	**la leonessa**
lizard	**la lucertola**
monkey	**la scimmia**
mouse	**il topo**
panda	**il panda**
panther	**la pantera**
raccoon	**il procione**
rat	**il ratto**

rattlesnake	il serpente a sonagli
rhinoceros	il rinoceronte
squirrel	lo scoiattolo
tiger	la tigre
trunk	la proboscide
wild	selvaggio; feroce
wolf	il lupo
zebra	la zebra

Fish, Creatures of the Sea, and Amphibians / I pesci, le creature del mare e gli anfibi

anemone	l(o)'anemone [di mare]
coral	il corallo
dolphin	il delfino
frog	la rana
school (of fish)	il branco (di pesci)
sea horse	il cavalluccio di mare
seal	la foca
shark	il pescecane/lo squalo
shell	la conchiglia
starfish	la stella di mare
toad	il rospo
whale	la balena

Birds / Gli uccelli

beak	il becco
condor	il condor
crane	la gru
crow	il corvo
down	le piume
duck	l(a)'anatra
eagle	l(a)'aquila
feather	la piuma; la penna
flamingo	il fenicottero
hawk	il falco
heron	l(o)'airone

migratory	**migratorio**
ostrich	**lo struzzo**
owl	**il gufo**
pelican	**il pellicano**
penguin	**il pinguino**
(bird) song	**il verso**
sparrow	**il passero**
stork	**la cicogna**
swallow	**la rondine**
swan	**il cigno**
vulture	**l(o)'avvoltoio**
wing	**l(a)'ala**
woodpecker	**il picchio**

Insects   Gli insetti

ant	**la formica**
bee	**l(a)'ape**
bumblebee	**il calabrone**
butterfly	**la farfalla**
cicada	**la cicala**
cockroach	**lo scarafaggio**
cricket	**il grillo**
dragonfly	**la libellula**
flea	**la pulce**
firefly	**la lucciola**
fly	**la mosca**
gnat	**il moscerino**
grasshopper	**la cavalletta**
locust	**la locusta**
mosquito	**la zanzara**
scorpion	**lo scorpione**
spider	**il ragno**
swarm	**lo sciame**
wasp	**la vespa**

12

Measures, Time, and Dates

Measurements and Quantities

Length and Width

La lunghezza e la larghezza

centimeter	**il centimetro**
decimeter	**il decimetro**
foot	**il piede**
inch	**il pollice**
kilometer	**il chilometro**
measure	**misurare; la misura**
meter	**il metro**

FF *I can't measure the door because I forgot the measuring tape.*

Non posso misurare la porta perché mi sono dimenticata il metro.

metric	**metrico**
mile	**il miglio**
millimeter	**il millimetro**
yard	**la iarda**

Volume and Weight

Il volume e il peso

deciliter	**il decilitro**
gallon	**il gallone**
gram	**il grammo**
gross	**[il peso] lordo**
kilogram	**il chilogrammo**
liter	**il litro**
net	**[il peso] netto**
ounce	**l(a)'oncia**
pint	**la pinta**
pound	**la libbra**
quart	**il quarto [di gallone]**
scale	**la bilancia; il peso**
tare	**la tara**
ton	**la tonnellata**

Numbers and Calculations

Cardinal Numbers	I numeri cardinali
zero	**zero**
one	**uno**

 Must-Know Tip

Numbers carry the article when they refer to the position they occupy in the numerical sequence, rather than the quantity they represent.

Zero is a fascinating number.	***Lo zero è un numero affascinante.***
One comes before two.	***L'uno viene prima del due.***

two	**due**
three	**tre**
four	**quattro**
five	**cinque**
six	**sei**
seven	**sette**
eight	**otto**
nine	**nove**
ten	**dieci**
eleven	**undici**
twelve	**dodici**
thirteen	**tredici**
fourteen	**quattordici**
fifteen	**quindici**
sixteen	**sedici**
seventeen	**diciassette**
eighteen	**diciotto**
nineteen	**diciannove**
twenty	**venti**

twenty-one	**ventuno**
twenty-two	**ventidue**
twenty-three	**ventitrè**
twenty-four	**ventiquattro**
twenty-five	**venticinque**
twenty-six	**ventisei**
twenty-seven	**ventisette**
twenty-eight	**ventotto**
twenty-nine	**ventinove**
thirty	**trenta**
forty	**quaranta**
fifty	**cinquanta**
sixty	**sessanta**
seventy	**settanta**
eighty	**ottanta**
ninety	**novanta**
one hundred; hundreds	**cento; il centinaio, [le] centinaia**
About a hundred dolphins lay dead on the shore.	*Un centinaio di delfini giacevano morti sul bagnasciuga.*
one hundred and one	**centouno**
two hundred	**duecento**
one thousand; thousands	**mille; il migliaio, [le] migliaia**
At the funeral, thousands of people filled the square.	*Al funerale, migliaia di persone riempirono la piazza.*
two thousand	**duemila**
ten thousand	**diecimila**
one hundred thousand	**centomila**
one million	**un milione**
two million	**due milioni**
The city spent two million euros to renovate the main square.	*Il comune ha speso due milioni di euro per restaurare la piazza principale.*
one billion	**un miliardo/un bilione**
one trillion	**un trilione**

count	contare; il calcolo
countless	innumerevole
decimal	[il] decimale
even	pari
figure; digit	la cifra; il numero
half	la metà
integer	l(o)'intero
myriad	una miriade di, miriadi di
negative	negativo
odd	dispari
positive	positivo
unique	[l(o)'] unico

Ordinal Numbers

I numeri ordinali

first

primo

First, let's agree on who is leading this group.

Primo, mettiamoci d'accordo su chi guida questo gruppo.

What are you having for your first course?

Che cosa prende di primo?

second

secondo

And for the second course?

E di secondo?

third

terzo

fourth	**quarto**
fifth	**quinto**
sixth	**sesto**
seventh	**settimo**
eighth	**ottavo**
ninth	**nono**
tenth	**decimo**
eleventh	**undicesimo**
twelfth	**dodicesimo**
thirteenth	**tredicesimo**
fourteenth	**quattordicesimo**
fifteenth	**quindicesimo**
sixteenth	**sedicesimo**
seventeenth	**diciassettesimo**
eighteenth	**diciottesimo**
nineteenth	**diciannovesimo**
twentieth	**ventesimo**
twenty-first	**ventunesimo**
twenty-second	**ventiduesimo**
twenty-third	**ventitreesimo**
twenty-fourth	**ventiquattresimo**
twenty-fifth	**venticinquesimo**
twenty-sixth	**ventiseiesimo**
twenty-seventh	**ventisettesimo**
twenty-eighth	**ventottesimo**
twenty-ninth	**ventinovesimo**
thirtieth	**trentesimo**
fortieth	**quarantesimo**
fiftieth	**cinquantesimo**
sixtieth	**sessantesimo**
seventieth	**settantesimo**
eightieth	**ottantesimo**
ninetieth	**novantesimo**
one hundredth	**centesimo**

one hundred first	**centunesimo/centounesimo**
two hundredth	**duecentesimo**
one thousandth	**millesimo**
ten thousandth	**decimillesimo**
one hundred thousandth	**centomillesimo**
one millionth	**milionesimo**

Mathematics and Geometry — La matematica e la geometria

add	**sommare; addizionare**
Addition: 3 plus 5 is 8.	*L'addizione: 3 più 5 fa 8.*
The sum of 3 and 5 is 8.	*La somma di 3 e 5 è 8.*
angle/corner	**l(o)'angolo**
area	**l(a)'area**
axiom	**l(o)'assioma**
axis	**l(o)'asse**
The horizontal axis is the X axis, and the vertical axis is the Y axis.	*L'asse 'X' [ics] è l'asse delle ascisse, e l'asse 'Y' [ipsilon] è quello delle ordinate.*
calculate	**calcolare**
circle	**il cerchio**
conversion	**la conversione**
cube	**il cubo**
cubic	**al cubo**
cylinder	**il cilindro**
demonstrate	**dimostrare**
diagonal	**[la] diagonale**
diameter	**il diametro**
divide	**dividere**
Division: 64 divided by 8 is 8.	*La divisione: 64 diviso 8 fa 8.*
double; twice	**[il] doppio; due volte**
equation	**l(a)'equazione**
equivalent	**l(a)'equivalenza**
example	**l(o)'esempio**
false	**falso**

fraction	**la frazione**
graph	**il grafico**
horizontal	**orizzontale**
hypothesis	**l(a)'ipotesi**
maximum	**[il] massimo**
minimum	**[il] minimo**
multiplication table	**la tavola pitagorica**
multiply	**moltiplicare**
Multiplication: 5 times 9 is 45.	***La moltiplicazione: 5 moltiplicato 9 fa 45.***
oblique	**obliquo**
opposite	**[l(o)'] opposto; il contrario**
parallel [to]	**parallelo [a]; la parallela**
perimeter	**il perimetro**
perpendicular	**[la] perpendicolare [a]**
polygon	**il poligono**
possibility	**la possibilità**
postulate	**il postulato**
power	**la potenza**
probability	**la probabilità**
proportion	**la proporzione**
prove	**provare; la prova**
quadruple	**[il] quadruplo; quattro volte**
radius	**il raggio**
Pi is the constant that allows us to calculate the circumference of a circle.	***Pi greco è la costante che permette di calcolare la circonferenza di un cerchio.***
ratio	**il rapporto**
rectangle	**il rettangolo**
result	**risultare; il risultato**
right/correct	**giusto**
root	**la radice**
We're learning to calculate a square root.	***Stiamo imparando a calcolare la radice quadrata.***
segment	**il segmento**
side	**il lato**

single	singolo
sphere	la sfera
square	il quadrato; al quadrato
straight line	la [linea] retta
subtract	sottrarre
Subtraction: 8 minus 2 is 6.	*La sottrazione: 8 meno 2 fa 6.*
tangent	[la] tangente [a]
theorem	il teorema
theory	la teoria
thesis	la tesi
total	fare il totale; il totale
triangle	il triangolo
triple/thrice	[il] triplo; tre volte
true	vero
vertical	[la] verticale
wrong	sbagliato

Physics, Biology, and Chemistry

La fisica, la biologia e la chimica

adaptation	l(o)'adattamento
atom	l(o)'atomo
cell	la cellula
chromosome	il cromosoma, i cromosomi
clone	il clone
DNA	il DNA (l'acido desossiribonucleico)
electron	(lo)'elettrone
element	l(o)'elemento
enzyme	l(o)'enzima, gli enzimi
evolution	l(a)'evoluzione
fact	[il] fatto
We must ascertain the facts, first of all.	*Bisogna accertare i fatti, prima di tutto.*
FF *This sweater is handmade.*	*Questo golf è fatto a mano.*
gaseous	gassoso

gene	**il gene**
genetics	**la genetica**
heredity	**l(a)'ereditarietà**
inorganic	**inorganico**
lever	**la leva**
liquid	**[il] liquido**
microscope	**il microscopio**
molecule	**la molecola**
natural laws	**le leggi naturali**
natural selection/survival of the fittest	**la selezione naturale**
neutron	**il neutrone**
organism	**l(o)'organismo**
particular	**particolare**
FF Vittorio isn't off-putting, but he's peculiar.	*Vittorio non è antipatico, ma è un tipo particolare.*
periodic table	**il sistema periodico**
phenomenon	**il fenomeno**
protein	**la proteina**
proton	**il protone**
quantum	**il quanto**
relative	**relativo**
relativity	**la relatività**
solid	**[il] solido**
tilt	**inclinare; l(a)'inclinazione**
universal	**universale**
vitamin	**la vitamina**

Time and the Calendar

Time

Il tempo

1940s	**gli anni quaranta**
1968	**il sessantotto**
Do you remember 1968, the year of the student revolution in Paris?	*Ti ricordi del sessantotto, l'anno della rivoluzione studentesca a Parigi?*

about/around	**circa/verso**
Shall we meet around seven?	*Ci vediamo verso le sette?*
A.D. (Anno Domini)/C.E. (Common Era)	**d.C. (dopo Cristo)**
again	**di nuovo; nuovamente**
ago	**fa**
already	**già**
always	**sempre**
at once	**subito**
B.C. (before Christ)	**a.C. (avanti Cristo)**
begin	**incominciare; iniziare**
beginning	**l(o)'inizio**
between the 18th and the 19th centuries	**tra il XVIII e il XIX secolo**
calendar	**il calendario**
century	**il secolo**

continue	**continuare**
date	**datare; la data**
day after tomorrow	**dopodomani**
day before yesterday	**l(o)'altro ieri**

duration	**la durata**
early/soon	**presto**
end	**finire; la fine**
His end was near.	*La sua fine era vicina.*
era	**l(a)'era; l(a)'epoca**
eternity	**l(a)'eternità**
ever; never	**mai; non... mai**
I've never seen him looking so good.	*Non l'ho mai visto così bene.*
every time	**ogni volta**
every other time	**una volta sì e una no**
finish	**finire**
Did she finish her project?	*Ha finito il suo progetto?*
following day	**l(o)'indomani**
former	**il primo; quello precedente**
from time to time	**di volta in volta; ogni tanto**
future	**[il] futuro**
immortality	**l(a)'immortalità**
in advance	**in anticipo**
in no time	**detto fatto**
in time	**in tempo**
I arrived in time for her speech!	*Sono arrivata in tempo per il suo discorso!*
just	**appena; solo/soltanto**
I made it just in time!	*Ce l'ho fatta appena in tempo!*
last	**durare; [l(o)'] ultimo; scorso**
In the latest issue of L'Espresso there was a long interview with Prodi.	*Nell'ultimo numero dell'Espresso c'era una lunga intervista con Prodi.*
We spent last weekend in Cortina.	*Abbiamo passato lo scorso weekend a Cortina.*
late	**tardi; in ritardo**
Hurry up, we're late!	*Sbrigati, siamo in ritardo!*
Are you late again?	*Hai fatto tardi un'altra volta?*
latter	**il secondo; quello seguente**
leap year	**l(o)'anno bisestile**
Louis X (Louis the Tenth)	**Luigi X (Luigi decimo)**

millennium	**il millennio**
nowadays	**oggigiorno**
often	**spesso**
once/one time	**una volta**
only	**solo; soltanto**
Do you only have skim milk?	*Ha solo il latte magro?*
on time	**in orario**
over	**sopra; finito**
The plane is flying over the mountains.	*L'aeroplano vola sopra le montagne.*
The war is over.	*La guerra è finita.*
next	**[il] prossimo**
We'll spend next weekend in Cortina.	*Passiamo il prossimo weekend a Cortina.*
Next stop, Greenwich Village.	*Prossima fermata, Greenwich Village.*
This coming Monday we will leave.	*Partiamo lunedì prossimo.*
past	**[il] passato**
penultimate/the one before last	**[il] penultimo**
period	**il periodo**
phase	**la fase**
present	**[il] presente**
rarely	**di rado/raramente**
sometimes	**qualche volta**
subsequent	**successivo**
suddenly	**improvvisamente**
still; yet	**ancora**
today	**oggi; al giorno d'oggi**
What day is today?	*Che giorno è oggi?*
tomorrow	**domani**
twice	**due volte**
year 1000	**l(o)'anno mille; il Mille**
year 2000	**il 2000/duemila**
yesterday	**ieri**

Holidays

I giorni festivi

All Saints' Day (November 1)	**Ognissanti/[Tutti] i Santi**
All Souls' Day (November 2)	**[Tutti] i Morti**

April 25; Liberation Day	**il 25 aprile; il Giorno della Liberazione**
On April 25, Italians celebrate the German surrender in World War II.	*Il 25 aprile, gli italiani celebrano la resa dei tedeschi nella Seconda guerra mondiale.*
Ascension	**[l(a)'] Ascensione**
Ash Wednesday	**[il] Mercoledì Santo**
August 15	**[il] Ferragosto**
On August 15, stores close, everyone goes on vacation, and the country shuts down.	*A Ferragosto, i negozi chiudono, tutti vanno in vacanza e il paese si ferma.*
Christmas Day	**[il] Natale**
In Italy, too, the Christmas tree is now more in fashion than the crèche, and Santa Claus more than the Christ Child.	*Anche in Italia ormai è di moda l'albero di Natale più del Presepe, e Babbo Natale più di Gesù Bambino.*
day after Christmas Day	**Santo Stefano**
Easter Monday	**Pasquetta**
Easter Sunday	**[la] Pasqua**
Good Friday	**[il] Venerdì Santo**
January 6	**l(a)'Epifania/la Befana**
July 4	**il 4 luglio; la Festa dell'Indipendenza**
June 2	**la Festa della Repubblica**
Labor Day	**Labor Day [la festa del lavoro]**
Lent	**[la] Quaresima**
Mardi Gras	**[il] Carnevale (Martedì Grasso)**
May 1/Workers' Day	**il Primo Maggio; la Festa dei Lavoratori**
New Year's Day	**[il] Capodanno**
New Year's Eve	**l'ultimo dell'anno/San Silvestro/la vigilia di Capodanno**
Pentecost	**[la] Pentecoste**
Thanksgiving	**il Giorno del Ringraziamento**
Valentine's Day	**il Giorno di San Valentino**

Italians have adopted several American holidays: Valentine's Day, Mother's Day, Father's Day, and Halloween.	*Gli italiani hanno adottato parecchie feste americane: il Giorno di San Valentino, il Giorno della Mamma, il Giorno del Papà, e Halloween.*

Telling Time   Dire l'ora

Do you have time?	*Hai tempo?*
Do you have the time?	*Hai l'ora?*
analogical	**analogico**
anymore/no more	**non più**
chronometer	**il cronometro**
clock	**l(o)'orologio [a muro]; il pendolo**
daylight saving time	**l'ora legale**
Cows have to be milked at the same time all year round, no matter whether it's standard time or daylight saving time.	*Le mucche vanno munte alla stessa ora tutto l'anno, che ci sia l'ora solare o l'ora legale.*
during	**durante**
face (of clock)	**il quadrante**
half/30 minutes	**mezza**
It's 10:30 A.M.	*Sono le dieci e mezza/trenta [di mattina].*
hand (of clock)	**la lancetta**
hour	**l(a)'ora**
What time is it?	*Che ora è?*
It's 1 o'clock A.M./P.M.	*È l'una [del pomeriggio; di notte].*
It's 2 o'clock P.M.	*Sono le due [del pomeriggio]./ Sono le 14.*
hourglass	**la clessidra**
midnight	**[la] mezzanotte**
It's midnight.	*È mezzanotte.*
minute	**[il] minuto**
I'll be with you in a minute!	*Sono con te tra un minuto.*
FF *She's a tiny girl.*	*È una bambina minuta.*
moment	**il momento; l(o)'attimo**

noon	[il] mezzogiorno
It's 12 noon.	È mezzogiorno./Sono le dodici.
It's 12:30 P.M.	È mezzogiorno e mezzo./È la mezza. (only for 12:30 P.M.)
pendulum	il pendolo
quarter/15 minutes	il quarto
It's 10:15.	Sono le dieci e un quarto/e quindici.
It's a quarter to 11.	Sono le undici meno un quarto.
quartz	[il] quarzo; al quarzo
second	[il] secondo
sundial	la meridiana
three quarters/45 minutes	tre quarti
It's 10:45.	Sono le dieci e tre quarti/e quarantacinque.
time zone	il fuso orario
watch	l(o)'orologio
watchband	il cinturino

Day and Night — Il giorno e la notte

afternoon	[il] pomeriggio
daily	giornalmente; quotidianamente; il [giornale] quotidiano
dark	[il] buio
dawn	l(a)'alba
day	la giornata; il giorno
Good day!/Good morning!	Buon giorno!

 Must-Know Tip

Giorno, **sera**, **notte**, and **anno** indicate a phase in the passing of time. **Giornata**, **serata**, **nottata**, and **annata** indicate a period of time. **Pomeriggio** and **secolo** indicate both a phase and a period of time.

Did you have a good day?	Hai passato una buona giornata?
We had a splendid evening.	La serata è stata splendida.
This past year has not been a good one for apples.	Questa non è stata un'annata buona per le mele.

day in, day out	con il passare dei giorni
evening	[la] sera; la serata
Good evening!	*Buona sera!*
every other day	un giorno sì e uno no
every third, fourth, etc., day	ogni tre, quattro, ecc., giorni
from day one	[fin] dal primo giorno
from day to day	di giorno in giorno
morning	il mattino, la mattina; la mattinata
night	la notte
Good night!	*Buona notte!*
overnight	dalla sera alla mattina
sunset	il tramonto
twilight	il crepuscolo; la penombra

Days of the Week — I giorni della settimana

Monday	[il] lunedì
Tuesday	[il] martedì
Wednesday	[il] mercoledì
Thursday	[il] giovedì
Friday	[il] venerdì
Saturday	[il] sabato
Sunday	[la] domenica
holiday	la festa; il giorno festivo; la festività, le festività
weekday	il giorno feriale
weekend	il fine settimana, i fine settimana; il weekend

Months of the Year — I mesi dell(o)'anno

January	[il] gennaio
February	[il] febbraio
March	[il] marzo
April	[l(o)'] aprile
May	[il] maggio

June	[il] giugno
July	[il] luglio
August	[l(o)'] agosto
September	[il] settembre
October	[l(o)'] ottobre
November	[il] novembre
December	[il] dicembre

 Must-Know Tip

In Italian, usually names of months are not accompanied by an article, unless they are accompanied by a qualifier.

In March you see the first violets.	*A marzo si vedono le prime violette.*
They were born in August.	*Sono nati ad agosto.*
In April 1945, . . .	*Nell'aprile del 1945...*
It was a rainy September.	*Fu un settembre piovoso.*

Exercises

The exercises that follow correspond to the units in this book. Exercise 5.2, for example, refers to vocabulary you encountered in Chapter 5. As in the rest of the book, the exercises are set up so you can focus on any subject area that interests you, such as shopping in Chapter 5, and move from one unit to another. Enjoy your practice!

1.1

Write the appropriate definite article for the following words. More than one article may be correct.

1. __la__ nascita

2. _____ telefono

3. _____ signore

4. _____ scuse

5. _____ domanda

6. _____ fax

7. _____ operatrice

8. _____ centralinista

9. _____ pagine gialle

10. _____ single

11. _____ direttore

12. _____ regalo

13. _____ Capodanno

14. _____ nomi

15. _____ cognome

16. _____ occupazione

17. _____ luoghi

18. _____ gaffe

19. _____ cellulari

20. _____ interno

1.2

Fill in the blanks by choosing one of the options listed below.

1. È al suo terzo _____, ma questa volta si sposa.

a. marito   b. fidanzata   c. fidanzato

2. Nostra madre è rimasta _____ a quarant'anni, e non si è più risposata.

a. vedova   b. divorziata   c. single

3. Quando si è sposata, Marta ha preso il nome del _____ .

a. fidanzato   b. vedova   c. marito

4. Signorina, deve aggiungere _____ al nome proprio.

a. il nome del marito   b. il suo cognome   c. il suo soprannome

1.3

Find the word that corresponds to each definition. Choose from among the words listed below.

addio   arrivederci   comportamento   domanda   favore
gentile   grazie   permesso   prego   scusa

1. Di chi ha maniere cortesi e amichevoli nei rapporti con gli altri.
   _____ (*adjective*)

2. Si usa come saluto nel separarsi da una persona o cosa cara.
   _____ (*interjection*)

3. Si usa come saluto nel prendere congedo da un persona con cui si ha confidenza. _____ (*interjection*)

4. Esprime ringraziamento, gratitudine, riconoscenza.
   _____ (*interjection*)

5. Interrogazione. _____ (*feminine noun*)

6. Modo di agire di un organismo animale o vegetale; condotta.
   _____ (*masculine noun*)

7. Si usa come formula di cortesia, rispondendo a chi ringrazia o chiede scusa, o per invitare qualcuno a sedersi, a entrare, ecc.
   _____ (*interjection*)

8. Parole, argomenti, atti e simili con cui si chiede di essere perdonati per un errore. _____ (*feminine noun*)

9. Formula di cortesia con cui si chiede di entrare o di passare.

_____ (*past participle*)

10. Azione che dimostra benevolenza verso qualcuno; aiuto.

_____ (*masculine noun*)

1.4

Match the answers to the correct questions.

_____ 1. Abito in Via Roma 54.   a. Le hai dato il nostro indirizzo?

_____ 2. Farò io le presentazioni.   b. Ciao, come va?

_____ 3. No, è andato via così in fretta!   c. Dove abiti?

_____ 4. No, ho chiesto alla Signorina   d. Hai chiesto alla Signora
        Mancini.   Cenci?

_____ 5. Non mi hanno ancora   e. Hai salutato suo marito?
        presentato.

_____ 6. Va bene, grazie.   f. Ti hanno presentato al Cardinale?

_____ 7. Gliel'ho dato ieri.   g. Chi farà le presentazioni?

1.5

Fill in the blanks, choosing from among the following words.

il centralino   il cordless   il telefonino   l'interno
messaggi   parlare   pronto   un numero verde

1. Quando fai _____ non paghi la telefonata.

2. Ha fatto il numero giusto, Signora, ma _____ è
cambiato.

3. _____ , chi parla?

4. I ragazzi comunicano solo più con _____ .

5. Hai visto dove ho messo _____ ?

6. Ho lasciato dieci _____ sulla segreteria telefonica di
Elena, ma non mi ha ancora risposto.

7. Posso _____ con Sara?

8. In ufficio, puoi chiamarlo direttamente a questo numero o tramite

_____ .

1.6

In the following sentences, replace the verb, choosing from among the following infinitives.

chiedere   mandare due righe   scusarsi (con)   regalare

ringraziare   salutare   telefonare (a)

1. Vogliono dare un quadro di Matisse alla nipote per il suo matrimonio.
2. Farete le vostre scuse alla segretaria?
3. Chiamano la mamma ogni giorno.
4. Sciverò una letterina a mia sorella.
5. Posso domandare un favore a tuo padre?
6. Dì buongiorno alla nonna!
7. Desiderano esprimere allo zio i loro ringraziamenti.

1.7

Add the appropriate interrogative word in Italian to each of the following sentences.

1. _____ vai al cinema?

2. _____ non hai accettato quel lavoro?

3. _____ vuoi mangiare per cena?

4. Sono partiti senza salutarti _____ non volevano svegliarti.

5. _____ va?

6. _____ vai? Vado alla stazione.

7. Non hai un'idea di _____ vino Giancarlo ha bevuto alla festa.

8. _____ cioccolatini hai mangiato?

9. Sai _____ mi ha detto?

10. _____ ha portato lo champagne?

11. Non so _____ hanno assunto.

12. Di _____ sono questi guanti?

1.8

Add the appropriate preposition to the following sentences. Choose from among: **di**, **a**, **da**, **in**, **con**, **su**, **per**, **fra/tra**, either in their simple forms or as **preposizioni articolate**.

1. Vado _____ casa.

2. Vuoi andare a teatro _____ me?

3. Ha fatto di tutto _____ suo figlio, inutilmente.

4. Mia cugina ha preso lezioni di violino _____ cinque anni, ma suona malissimo.

5. Il gatto è saltato _____ tavolo e ha mangiato la bistecca.

6. La scopa è _____ cucina.

7. Vengono _____ Svezia.

8. Non lo vede _____ tre anni.

9. Il giornale è caduto _____ il mobile e la finestra.

10. Il giornale _____ ieri riportava la notizia dell'incidente.

1.9

For each Italian word, circle its English translation.

1. accettare
   a. to write   b. to offer   c. to accept

2. l'invito
   a. inauguration   b. invitation   c. occasion

3. l'appuntamento
   a. appointment   b. announcement   c. reception

4. la cartolina
   a. postcard   b. envelope   c. letter

5. il francobollo
   a. mail box   b. reception   c. stamp

6. la lettera
   a. gift   b. postcard   c. letter

7. il mittente
a. address
b. sender
c. mailperson

8. scrivere
a. to write
b. to refuse
c. to wish

9. spedire
a. to accept
b. to receive
c. to ship

2.1

Decide whether the following statements are correct or not by writing Yes or No next to each one.

_____ 1. Nelle favole la principessa è sempre carina.

_____ 2. Le persone anziane spesso hanno le rughe.

_____ 3. L'espressione del viso diventa allegra quando si piange.

_____ 4. Gli occhi chiari sono più sensibili alla luce.

_____ 5. Se hai i capelli corti puoi fare le trecce.

_____ 6. I capelli biondi sono tipici dei popoli scandinavi.

_____ 7. I capelli ricci sono tipici dei popoli scandinavi.

2.2

Insert the proper verb in each of the following sentences. Use the simple present tense.

1. Mia figlia _____ (resembles) tutta suo padre: ha i suoi occhi, il suo viso e il suo sorriso.

2. I bambini non hanno ancora telefonato! Hanno detto che andavano dalla zia! Non _____ (worry [you, sing.]), vedrai che si faranno vivi tra poco.

3. Ti _____ (like) il gelato al cioccolato? Mi _____ (like) moltissimo, ma ne devo mangiarne poco, se no sto male.

4. Carlo e Valeria non _____ (know) se i loro amici vengono con tutti i figli, o solo con le due figlie maggiori.

5. I miei genitori _____ (know) il mio fidanzato da molti anni, ma non si sentono a loro agio con lui.

6. Che noia! Devo dire le cose non una, ma due o tre volte, perché lui _____ (thinks) sempre ad altro.

7. Hai bisogno di aiuto? No, credo di riuscire a _____ (manage) da solo.

8. _____ (understand [you, pl.]) che cosa sta dicendo? No, parla una lingua che nessuno di noi ha mai sentito.

2.3

Add the appropriate verbs to the following sentences. Choose from among **dovere**, **lasciare**, **potere**, **sapere**, and **volere** (must/have to, let, can/may, know, will). Use the simple present tense.

1. Mi ha offeso così profondamente che non _____ vederli mai più.

2. _____ (third-person sing.) fare di tutto.

3. Ma i nostri vicini _____ proprio fare rumore tutta la notte?

4. Mi _____ aiutare i vostri genitori?

5. Solo persone molto intelligenti _____ apprezzare quello che hai fatto per il paese.

2.4

Add the noun conveying the appropriate kinship relation.

1. Il fratello di mio padre è mio _____ .

2. I figli di suo fratello sono i suoi _____ .

3. Il marito di tua sorella è tuo _____ .

4. La madre di suo marito è sua _____ .

5. I genitori di mia moglie sono i miei _____ .

6. Considero il figlio di mio marito come se fosse mio _____ .

7. Tua figlia è la _____ di tua madre.

8. L'altra figlia di sua madre è sua _____ .

9. Abbiamo visto tutti i _____ al matrimonio.

10. Suo marito l'ha lasciata per l'_____ .

11. La moglie di mio fratello è la _____ dei miei figli.

12. Massimo e Sandra hanno cinque _____ .

2.5

Write the word that is the opposite of the following adjectives.

1. bello/ _____

2. alto/ _____

3. cattivo/ _____

4. debole/ _____

5. triste/ _____

6. intelligente/ _____

2.6

Assign the auxiliary **essere** or **avere** to the following verbs.

1. _____ accorgersi

2. _____ adorare

3. _____ amare

4. _____ ammirare

5. _____ aspettare

6. _____ avere

7. _____ capire

8. _____ cavarsela

9. _____ credere

10. _____ decidere

11. _____ dimenticarsi

12. _____ diventare

13. _____ essere

14. _____ fare

15. _____ frequentare

16. _____ incontrare

17. _____ promettere

18. _____ ricordare

19. _____ ricordarsi

20. _____ sapere

21. _____ sentirsi   23. _____ sperare

22. _____ sfogarsi   24. _____ sposarsi

3.1

Match the names for parts of the body that follow with the functions below. Not all names of body parts are used.

gli occhi   i fianchi   le braccia   il cervello   il collo

il naso   il petto   il polso   la bocca   la coscia

la faccia   la fronte   la gola   la lingua   la mano

la pancia   la testa   la vita   le dita   le ginocchia

le gambe   le mani   le orecchie   lo stomaco

1. abbracciare _____

2. correre _____

3. digerire _____

4. inginocchiarsi _____

5. mangiare _____

6. pensare _____

7. acchiappare _____

8. scrivere _____

9. sentire _____

10. vedere _____

3.2

Choose from among the appropriate verbs to complete the sentences listed below.

ascoltare   assaggiare   baciare   camminare

digerire   guardare   indicare   masticare

sentire   toccare   vedere

1. Usiamo le gambe per _____ .

2. I denti servono a _____ .

3. Il proverbio dice: '_____ e non _____ !'

4. Se sei sordo non puoi _____ .

5. Con la bocca si può _____ .

6. Che piacere per le mie orecchie, _____ della buona musica.

7. Si usa la lingua per _____ .

8. Se mangi troppo in fretta, diventa più difficile _____ .

9. Che dito si usa per _____ ?

10. Non lo voglio _____ mai più!

3.3

Indicate if the following statements are true or false, reasonable or unreasonable, by writing Yes or No next to each one.

_____ 1. Il colesterolo alto dipende solo dalla dieta.

_____ 2. I vegani non mangiano neanche le uova.

_____ 3. Non si è mai troppo magri.

_____ 4. Bisogna pesarsi tre volte al giorno.

_____ 5. Nella dieta macrobiotica si mangiano molte verdure.

_____ 6. Il fast food fa bene ai bambini.

3.4

English is now the lingua franca of the entire world, especially in the tourist business. Here follows a conversation between an American tourist who has to rush to the hospital and the people he encounters in his attempt to reach it, and when he tries to explain what he needs. Insert the appropriate Italian and English words.

Tourist: Sir, Sir, can you help me find the nearest hospital?

Passerby: Hos... che? Hotel?

Tourist: No, no, H-O-S-P-I-T-A-L, where you go when you're sick! [grimacing to show pain]

Passerby: Ah, (1) _____ ! Ma sta male? Ha bisogno di aiuto?

Tourist: Aito?

Passerby: No, aiuto! [Gently taking the other man by an elbow as if to support him.]

Tourist: I see, do I need (2) _____ ? No, just directions.

Passerby: Continui dritto per due isolati, poi giri a sinistra. In fondo al viale, vedrà l'ospedale.

Tourist [gratefully]: (3) _____ !

Passerby: (4) _____ !

About ten minutes later, the tourist arrives at the doors of the ER. He walks into the hall and staggers, almost falling. A nurse runs toward him and calls for a doctor. A physician arrives a few minutes later.

Doctor: Dobbiamo assicurarci che non ci sia qualche problema al cuore.

Tourist: Cu... ore?

Doctor: Non si preoccupi. Per escludere un (5) _____ , facciamo un elettrocardiogramma.

Doctor: Adesso la ricoveriamo, così posso fare tutti gli (6) _____ necessari.

Tourist: Do you mean tests?

Doctor: Sì, faccio un prelievo di sangue e un (7) _____ delle urine.

3.5

Here follows a list of words with definitions listed below. Match each word with the appropriate definition.

adolescenza   bene   bocca   cura   dentista

diabete   dieta   donna   guarire   magro

male   mano   morire   rene   sano

testa   vena   vita

1. Sottile, senza grassi. _____ (*male adjective*)

2. In modo giusto, buono. _____ (*adverb*)

3. In modo non buono, non giusto. _____ (*adverb*)

4. Età della vita tra la fanciullezza e l'età adulta, caratterizzata dalla maturazione sessuale. _____ (*feminine noun*)

5. Segmento dell'arto superiore che comprende il palmo e le dita. _____ (*feminine noun*)

6. Cavità della parte inferiore della testa, limitata dalle labbra, è sede del gusto e, nell'uomo, della parola. _____ (*feminine noun*)

7. Femmina adulta della specie umana. _____ (*feminine noun*)

8. Insieme delle terapie e dei medicamenti usato per il trattamento di una malattia. _____ (*feminine noun*)

9. Parte del corpo che in uomini e animali contiene il cervello, la parte superiore dell'apparato digerente e diversi organi di senso. _____ (*feminine noun*)

10. Regime alimentare a fini terapeutici o dimagranti. _____ (*feminine noun*)

11. Spazio di tempo compreso tra la nascita e la morte. _____ (*feminine noun*)

12. Vaso sanguigno che conduce il sangue al cuore. _____ (*feminine noun*)

13. Ciascuna delle due ghiandole aventi la funzione di secernere l'urina. _____ (*masculine noun*)

14. Che è senza malattie e disturbi; che gode di buona salute. _____ (*adjective*)

15. Malattia causata dall'insufficiente secrezione di insulina. _____ (*masculine noun*)

16. Medico specialista nella cura delle malattie dentarie. _____ (*masculine noun*)

17. Cessare di vivere. _____ (*intransitive verb*)

18. a. Risanare, riportare in salute   b. Rimettersi in salute. _____ (*transitive or intransitive verb*)

3.6

From the right column, pair the word that is either the opposite or the complementary one with the appropriate word in the left column.

_____ 1. omosessuale		a. grasso
_____ 2. uomo		b. giovinezza
_____ 3. magro		c. sinistra
_____ 4. vecchiaia		d. tirare
_____ 5. nascere		e. donna
_____ 6. ammalato		f. eterosessuale
_____ 7. piangere		g. morire
_____ 8. spingere		h. ridere
_____ 9. destra		i. sano

3.7

Order the following series of words in the logical sequence.

1. morire, crescere, nascere, invecchiare

   _____ , _____ , _____ ,

   _____

2. seppellire, allattare, dare alla luce, tirare su

   _____ , _____ , _____ ,

   _____

3. anziano, adulto, giovane, di mezza età

   _____ , _____ , _____ ,

   _____

4. pubertà, vecchiaia, adolescenza, infanzia

   _____ , _____ , _____ ,

   _____

4.1

Circle the words with their English equivalents.

1. i compiti a casa
   a. homework   b. mistake   c. nursery school

2. ignorante
a. easy   b. correct   c. ignorant

3. il liceo
a. professional school   b. lyceum   c. elementary school

4. imparare
a. explain   b. learn   c. update

5. insegnare
a. read   b. promote   c. teach

6. l'anno scolastico
a. school year   b. middle school   c. pass

7. l'errore
a. mistake   b. talent   c. study

8. la studentessa
a. childhood   b. female student c. student

9. la dote
a. degree   b. talent   c. education

10. il supplente
a. teacher   b. principal   c. substitute teacher

4.2

Write the English equivalent for each of the following words.

1. avere un crash _____

2. cliccare _____

3. fare un backup _____

4. il click _____

5. il dischetto _____

6. il portatile _____

7. l'intelligenza artificiale _____

8. l'interfaccia _____

9. la memoria _____

10. la pila _____

11. la videata _____

12. riavviare il sistema _____

4.3

The following words are all related to various aspects of the educational process. Group them according to the category below, to which they belong.

agraria   copiare   dare il voto   discutere la tesi   fare l'appello

fare lezione   il conservatorio   il corso   il dipartimento

il politecnico   il rettore   il ricercatore   il seminario

il voto insegnare   iscriversi all'università   l'abilitazione

l'amministrazione aziendale   l'educazione civica l'esame

l'esame di ammissione   l'esame di stato   l'insegnante   la biblioteca

la bibliotecaria   la biologia   la geometria   la giurisprudenza

la laurea   la maestra   la medicina   la pagella

la psicologia   laurearsi   le tasse universitarie

ritirarsi da un corso   tagliare

1. disciplines: _____

   _____

2. degrees and certifications: _____

   _____

3. professions and roles in the field of education and research:

   _____

   _____

4. activities and institutions: _____

   _____

5. actions: _____

   _____

4.4

Choose the sentence that explains the function of each of the following items or actions.

_____ 1. il motore di ricerca

   a. serve a controllare la memoria del computer

   b. aiuta a svolgere ricerche sull'Internet

   c. fa ripartire il computer dopo un crash

   d. spiega perché bisogna fare una ricerca col computer

_____ 2. la casella di posta elettronica

   a. è una casella postale che si apre con un codice elettronico

   b. è una buca delle lettere che si apre e si chiude elettronicamente

   c. è un indirizzo virtuale dove si ricevono i messaggi elettronici

   d. è un piccolo ufficio postale riservato a clienti con codice di accesso elettronico

_____ 3. quando masterizzi un CD

   a. copi dei dati da una fonte elettronica ad un dischetto

   b. rendi utilizzabile un CD mai usato prima

   c. inserisci un codice che permette l'uso del CD solo a chi ne è in possesso

   d. scopri il codice che ti consente di leggere un CD

_____ 4. personalizzare vuol dire

   a. prendere le cose troppo sul serio

   b. appropriarsi di qualcosa che non ti appartiene

   c. adattare un programma alle necessità ed ai gusti di una persona o di un gruppo

   d. essere troppo adattabile ed arrendevole

_____ 5. il supporto interattivo è

a. l'aiuto reciproco tra i membri di un gruppo

b. una terapia psicologica basata su attività di gruppo

c. un meccanismo che sostituisce una componente di un sistema che ha smesso di funzionare

d. un sistema di software che consente all'utente di ottenere consigli e informazioni via Internet

5.1

Fill in the blanks by choosing the appropriate label, method of payment, or transaction among the ones suggested below each phrase.

1. Il consumismo spinge la gente a comprare articoli
   _____ .

a. lo status symbol   b. di lusso   c. all'ingrosso

2. Il commerciante mi ha convinto a comprare la pelliccia facendomi un bello _____ .

a. vendita   b. ordine   c. sconto

3. Vorrei _____ cento dollari in euro.

a. comprare   b. aumentare   c. cambiare

4. Non accettiamo _____ ; solo contanti e assegni.

a. carte di credito   b. traveler's cheques   c. assegni

5. Mia zia ha comprato un televisore _____ ; finirà di pagarlo tra un anno.

a. al dettaglio   b. in contanti   c. a rate

5.2

You're a fashion consultant. Help a client choose her clothes from the list for the activities and occasions listed below.

1. blue jeans
2. gonna di lana a pieghe
3. T-shirt
4. un abito da sera lungo di seta rossa
5. un anello di diamanti
6. una borsetta nera e una marrone

7. un cardigan di lana pesante
8. un completo di lana arancione
9. un golfino di cashmere
10. un impermeabile rosso scuro
11. un ombrello grigio a righe nere
12. un paio di orecchini in acciaio
13. un paio di pantaloni di tweed marroni e verdi
14. un paio di pantofole rosse
15. un vestito di lana blu
16. una borsetta da sera
17. una camicetta bianca, tipo camicia da uomo
18. una camicetta di cotone bianca a righe blu ed una rossa a righe bianche
19. una cintura marrone ed una nera
20. una collana in acciaio
21. una giacca di velluto blu elettrico
22. una minigonna di pelle nera
23. una spilla anni quaranta di platino con perle
24. uno scialle a disegni cashmere

a. a week-long business trip in March: _____

b. a weekend in the countryside in November: _____

c. a relaxing, though slightly cold, winter afternoon at home: _____

_____

d. opening night at the opera in October: _____

e. a dinner out with friends in a trendy restaurant: _____

5.3

Here follow garments from a fashion show. Answer the questions following each item.

Sfilata di moda uomo autunno inverno 2006

1. What kind of show are you reading about?_____

2. For what season?_____

Brunello Cucinelli: Brunello Cucinelli propone un blazer giovane, informale ma elegante, con la giacca a righe e i pantaloni sportivi.

3. Is this outfit meant for a young, middle-aged, or elderly man?

   _____

4. Is it meant to be formal or informal? _____

5. How is the jacket described? _____

6. How are the trousers described? _____

Paul & Shark: Il giaccone Alaska di Paul & Shark, venduto insieme alla tenda, è stato pensato per gli appassionati dello sport estremo: ha l'imbottito in piuma d'oca e l'esterno idrorepellente, che permettono di affrontare le temperature più basse senza problemi.

7. What's the name of this garment? _____

8. What is it sold with? _____

9. What material is it filled with? _____

10. What is the main feature of its exterior fabric? _____

11. What would the person who wears it be able to do? _____

    _____

Entomology: Maurizio Freschi ha messo il logo e l'indirizzo delle università di entomologia più famose del mondo—New York, Miami, Copenhagen—sulle sue T-shirt in cotone o in jersey, completate da golfini, felpe e borse: un omaggio al piccolo grande mondo delle formiche.

12. What is the source of inspiration for this garment?

    _____

13. What materials can this garment be made of? _____

14. What other items are produced that look similar to the T-shirts?

    _____

15. What is their distinctive feature? _____

5.4

In the following sentences, replace the noun referring to the store with the noun that indicates the profession of the owner/manager or vice versa. Replace the preposition accordingly.

Example: Sono in tabaccheria. → Sono dal tabaccaio.

1. Sono dal farmacista. _____

2. Sono andati dal lattaio. _____

3. Entriamo nel negozio di frutta e verdura. _____

4. Passano tutti i pomeriggi dal gelataio. _____

5. Sono passata per caso in gioielleria. _____

6. Dal salumaio c'era troppa gente. _____

7. Hai chiesto dal droghiere? _____

6.1

Complete the following sentences choosing the appropriate dwelling or feature.

1. Se vivi al trentacinquesimo piano, vivi in _____.

2. Fuori ci sono 30 gradi (centigradi) e dentro ce ne sono 20. Sei in un edificio con _____.

3. Ecco perché chiedono così poco d'affitto per quel grande appartamento! È al quinto piano _____.

4. Va a vivere _____ perché vuole allevare polli e conigli.

5. Ci siamo messi insieme ad altre venti famiglie e abbiamo formato _____.

6. Mia zia è sempre vissuta _____ città, dove ci sono i buoni ristoranti, i negozi di lusso e i musei.

7. Ci mancava solo lo schnautzer, dai vicini. E non hanno neanche messo il cartello '_____'!

8. Mi sono chiusa fuori casa. Ma dove ho messo _____?

9. Come hai fatto a impolverarti in quel modo? Sono andata _____ a cercare i nostri vecchi giocattoli.

10. Tutti i vicini si sono lamentati: d'ora in poi ai bambini è permesso giocare _____ solo dalle 4 alle 7 del pomeriggio.

11. Vi interessa comprare _____? Non è cara, arriva smontata, viene montata sul posto in pochi giorni ed è esattamente come la volete.

6.2

You are helping a manager from your firm move to Rome and find a place to buy. Write an ad. The questions below will help you find the words you need in unit 6.

Example: Inserzione: Cercasi appartamento in zona centrale, quattro camere da letto, salone, cucina abitabile (*eat-in kitchen*), due bagni, garage, etc.

Ad: Do you want a single-family dwelling in Rome? in a semicentral neighborhood, but close to a park and schools for kids? a two-car garage? a garden? a large kitchen? four bedrooms? three bathrooms? a fixed mortgage? thirty percent down (*caparra*)?

_____

_____

_____

6.3

You are an interior decorator who is suggesting materials and furniture to a client. Assign the appropriate materials and pieces of furniture to each room.

1. Se volete una camera da letto semplice, questo _____ basso di stile giapponese è l'ideale.

a. letto   b. guardaroba   c. specchio

2. Mi avete detto che non vi piace la moquette. Allora in soggiorno possiamo mettere _____ di quercia.

a. il marmo   b. le piastrelle c. il parquet

3. Per le camere dei bambini, sceglierei una _____ con dei disegni allegri e colorati.

a. tinta   b. tappezzeria c. scrivania

6.4

Choose the appropriate verb to complete the following sentences. Use the infinitive or the gerund.

1. In genere, in camera da letto si va a _____ .

a. apparecchiare   b. entrare   c. dormire

2. Se vuoi che qualcuno si sieda, dici: "La prego di _____ ."

a. svegliarsi   b. accomodarsi   c. chiudersi.

3. Stavo _____ , quando ho inciampato, ho saltato sei gradini e sono caduto.

a. avendo un incubo   b. scendendo le scale c. riparando la lavatrice

4. Se vuoi _____ una cena veramente completa, hai bisogno di due forni.

a. cucinare   b. riscaldare   c. comprare

5. La mamma ti ha detto di _____ prima di andare a scuola.

a. far da mangiare   b. spegnere le luci   c. rifare il letto

6.5

Find the opposite of the following verbs.

1. accendere/ _____

2. addormentarsi/ _____

3. alzarsi (after sleeping)/ _____

4. chiudere/ _____

5. comprare/ _____

6. congelare/ _____

7. scendere le scale/ _____

8. sparecchiare/ _____

9. sporcare/ _____

10. uscire/ _____

6.6

You are having dinner in Rome with three friends who do not speak Italian. On a separate piece of paper, translate the parts of the menu below for them.

I primi

Spaghetti alla carbonara
Conditi con un soffritto di pancetta, aglio, olio d'oliva, vino bianco secco, uova, parmigiano e prezzemolo tritato

Farfalle della nonna
Con un sugo alla panna con cipolla rossa, rosmarino, gorgonzola e noci

Fettuccine di pasta fresca alla genovese
Con una salsa al pesto con gamberetti, peperoni arrostiti e pomodori pelati

Risotto ai frutti di mare
Con i gamberetti in un soffritto di olio d'oliva e aglio

Gnocchi ai tre formaggi
Gnocchi di patate conditi con fontina, gorgonzola, parmigiano e un sugo di burro e salvia

Desserts

Tiramisu
Savoiardi (*ladyfingers*) bagnati in caffè e rum, ricoperti con una crema all'uovo, cacao e zucchero.

Misto bosco (wild berries)
Lamponi, fragole e mirtilli al vino bianco secco frizzante e zucchero

Macedonia di frutta
Uva, banane, pesche, albicocche, kiwi e ananas con succo di limone/lime e zucchero

7.1

You will find below a detailed list of sectors in which jobs are offered. Match the brief descriptions of people, their credentials, qualifications, and work experience to the appropriate sector. One person's CV may match more than one sector.

agricoltura   altre attività   ambiente/ecologia   amministrazione artigianato

attività commerciali   credito/assicurazioni   editoria   finanza

franchising   industria   informatica   Internet   libere professioni

lingue   management   marketing   pubblicità   pubblico impiego

sanità   spettacolo   telecomunicazioni   turismo

1. Giulia Olivari ha conseguito (*has been awarded a degree in*) la Laurea in Giurisprudenza nel 1989, all'Università La Sapienza di Roma, con la votazione di 110 su 110 e lode. Nel 1990 ha fatto uno stage di sei mesi presso l'*International Labour Organization, The United Nations,* Ginevra. Tra il 1991 e il 2003 è stata responsabile di vari settori dell'*Ufficio rapporti con la pubblica amministrazione* di una grande società edilizia pubblica e commerciale (edilizia non residenziale). Dal 2002 a oggi è

stata dirigente dello stesso ufficio. Ha svolto le seguenti mansioni: stesura e controllo di contratti di appalto; negoziati con organizzazioni sindacali; controllo finanziario dei subappalti; preparazione dei bilanci. Parla e scrive correntemente l'inglese.

2. Patrizia Morra si è laureata in Storia moderna, Facoltà di Lettere e Filosofia, Università Statale di Milano, nel 1977. Tra il 1978 e il 1979 ha fatto un'esperienza di giornalismo presso un piccolo quotidiano di Bergamo. Dal 1979 al 1981 è stata scrittrice di testi per le trasmissioni culturali di NuovaTV, una rete televisiva privata. Dal 1981 al 1985 è stata insegnante supplente di Lettere (Italiano, Latino, Storia, Geografia) nella scuola media inferiore; dal 1986 al 2002, insegnante di ruolo [*tenured*] di Lettere (Italiano, Latino, Storia, Geografia) nella scuola media inferiore. Dal 2002 è casalinga (per occuparsi della famiglia e dei figli). Ha un'ottima conoscenza del tedesco e una buona conoscenza del francese. Pensionata dalla scuola, desidera un'occupazione a tempo parziale o a tempo pieno, non nell'insegnamento.

7.2

Match the following job offers with the appropriate sector from the previous exercise.

1. addetta rapporti commerciali _____

2. agente editoria e pubblicità multimediale _____

3. analisti programmatori _____

4. guida turistica _____

5. commesso/a _____

6. avvocato diritti d'impresa _____

7. buyer per catena di grandi magazzini _____

8. call marketing center _____

9. consulente del benessere _____

10. consulenti globali sanitari _____

11. esperto paghe e contributi _____

12. giardiniere _____

13. Greenpeace cerca consulenti su Firenze e Roma _____

14. impiegato ufficio tecnico _____

15. informatico _____

16. operatore multilingue, grande azienda finanziaria _____

17. programmatori pagine web _____

18. promotore finanziario _____

19. ragioniera _____

20. restauratore _____

21. scrittori/editori _____

22. sviluppo software _____

23. tecnico monitoraggio ambientale _____

24. igienista _____

7.3

The following chart shows a subsector of Italian firms. Answer the questions below.

Società italiane che offrono opzioni di partecipazione azionaria ai loro dirigenti

	Numero	Percentuale
Società italiane quotate in borsa in Italia	88	28,02%
Società italiane quotate all'estero	8	2,54%
Totale delle società italiane quotate in borsa	96	30,57%
Società italiane non quotate in borsa	122	38,85%
Totale	314	99,98%

1. Does the chart above regard publicly traded firms only?

   _____

2. Does it include foreign firms? _____

3. How many firms of the type considered here are publicly traded outside Italy? _____

4. Are there more private or public firms in this sector in Italy?

_____

5. What subsector of Italian firms does this chart take into consideration?

_____

6. What firms represent the highest percentage of these kinds of firms, private or public? _____

7.4

What follows is a brief history of Fiat, the Italian automotive company. Fill in the gaps, by choosing among the following words.

accordo Automobili automobili azionista boom

design Direttore economici estero

Europa fabbrica lavoratori logo mercato

modelli personale pista produzione scioperi sindacato

stabilimenti tecnico tradizione veicoli

La storia della Fiat è incominciata molti anni fa, all'alba del processo di industrializzazione in Italia, nel quale la società ha sempre svolto un ruolo primario. Il (1) _____ 'FIAT' ha un notevole valore simbolico, non solo per le macchine che l'azienda produce, ma perché simboleggia una (2) _____ di lavoro e di contributo allo sviluppo della società italiana.

La Fiat venne lanciata l'11 luglio 1899 a Torino, con il nome 'Società Anonima (3) _____ Italiana Automobili Torino'. Il maggiore (4) _____ era Giovanni Agnelli che divenne il primo (5) _____ Generale dell'azienda. La prima fabbrica venne costruita nel quartiere del Lingotto tra il 1916 e il 1922: era all'epoca la più grande d' (6) _____ e divenne famosa soprattutto per la (7) _____ di prova delle macchine sul tetto.

Durante il fascismo e la seconda guerra mondiale, la produzione di (8) _____ diminuì, mentre crebbe quella di (9) _____ commerciali e ferroviari.

Negli anni sessanta il (10) _____ economico condusse a
una notevole crescita sia del (11) _____ interno, sia di
quello (12) _____ . Fu anche un periodo di grossi scontri
con il (13) _____ , con molti (14) _____ e
notevoli miglioramenti (15) _____ e di trattamento per i
(16) _____ . La Fiat incominciò anche a costruire (17)
_____ nel Sud Italia. Nel 1978 venne creato il sistema
'Robogate' che automatizzò gran parte della (18) _____ alla
catena di montaggio.

Negli ultimi anni, la società ha conosciuto un periodo di crisi che l'ha
portata a ridurre notevolmente il (19) _____ .
L'(20) _____ con la General Motors è stato revocato. Di
recente, la Fiat ha proposto nuovi (21) _____ , che sono
innovativi sia dal punto di vista del (22) _____ sia dal
punto di vista (23) _____ .

7.5

Match the words that correspond to the following definitions.

gestire   il costo   la domanda   il cambio   il brevetto

il bilancio   l'economia   economico   l'efficienza   la produttività

multinazionale   la concorrenza   la ripresa   la valuta

la finanza   l'inflazione   l'offerta   il monopolio

1. Calcolo delle entrate e delle uscite relativo a un dato periodo nella
   gestione di un'azienda. _____ (*masculine noun*)

2. Certificato ufficiale della paternità di un'invenzione.
   _____ (*masculine noun*)

3. Operazione di scambio di una moneta con un'altra.
   _____ (*masculine noun*)

4. Condizione di mercato nella quale ogni operatore economico ha la
   stessa possibilità di offrire beni e servizi. _____
   (*feminine noun*)

5. Spesa che bisogna sostenere per ottenere qualcosa.
   _____ (*masculine noun*)

6. a. Interrogazione; quesito. b. Quantità richiesta di un dato bene.
   _____ (feminine noun)

7. L'insieme della attività e dei rapporti fra uomini connessi alla produzione, alla distribuzione e al consumo di beni e servizi.
   _____ (feminine noun)

8. a. Relativo all'economia. b. Poco costoso. _____
   (masculine adjective)

9. Capacità di raggiungere un risultato al livello massimo possibile di produttività. _____ (feminine noun)

10. Attività di raccolta dei mezzi e del loro impiego in imprese economiche. _____ (feminine noun)

11. Amministrare un'impresa. _____ (transitive verb)

12. Processo di costante aumento dei prezzi che porta al declino del potere d'acquisto. _____ (feminine noun)

13. Regime di mercato in cui un prodotto o servizio è fornito da un solo operatore economico. _____ (masculine noun)

14. Grande società industriale, commerciale o bancaria che mantiene il centro direttivo in un paese, ma ha importanti attività produttive in vari paesi del mondo. _____
    (feminine noun)

15. Messa a disposizione di beni e servizi sul mercato.
    _____ (feminine noun)

16. Rapporto tra fattori di produzione e prodotto che indica il grado di efficienza dei fattori impiegati in un processo produttivo.
    _____ (feminine noun)

17. La fase positiva di un ciclo economico, successiva a una recessione.
    _____ (feminine noun)

18. Moneta circolante in un paese. _____ (feminine noun)

8.1

Name the appropriate activity or profession the group of children below declare they want to pursue when they have grown up. *Example:*

Da grande voglio fare...   *When I grow up I want to be . . .*

Da grande voglio fare l'astronauta!   *When I grow up I want to be an astronaut!*

1. Michele: quello che fa passare i leoni attraverso il cerchio di fuoco!

   _____

2. Sandro: quello che suona lo strumento con tutti quei tasti bianchi e neri! _____

3. Silvia: quella che racconta le notizie alla televisione!

   _____

4. Susanna: quella che sta sempre sulle punte!

   _____

5. Ottavia: quello che fa volare in aria tante palline!

   _____

6. Massimo: quello con la bacchetta che dà gli ordini a tanti strumenti!

   _____

7. Elisa: quella che recita nei film! _____

8. Luigi: quello che sta seduto e guarda gli show!

   _____

9. Piero: quello che racconta la partita di calcio alla radio!

   _____

10. Gianni e Anna: quelli che si lanciano dal trampolino e si prendono al volo a mezz'aria! _____

11. Bobo: quello che fa ridere tutti al circo! _____

12. Carlo: quello che sceglie i pezzi di musica e fa ballare la gente!

    _____

13. Giulia: quella che posa per il pittore! _____

14. Daniele: quello che disegna le case! _____

15. Giacomo: quello che fa girare la ruota e modella la creta!

_____

16. Donatella: quella che cammina sul filo! _____

8.2

It is opening night for your new big musical on Broadway. You are the impresario. The story is set during Carnival, with actors wearing masks and holding puppets. Decide whether the following statements are True or False.

_____ 1. Hai bisogno di un circo.

_____ 2. Devi far disegnare delle maschere.

_____ 3. Bastano tre musicisti.

_____ 4. Lo spettacolo si svolge nell'orchestra.

_____ 5. Il corpo di ballo ha scritto la sceneggiatura.

_____ 6. Hai bisogno di costumi.

_____ 7. Assumi molti attori.

_____ 8. I burattini compongono il coro.

8.3

Here follow items artists need to create their work. Match each artist with the appropriate phrase.

Example: Il vasaio modella un vaso di ceramica. _The potter molds a ceramic vase._

_____ 1. il compositore | a. recita le sue poesie

_____ 2. il narratore | b. prende delle fotografie in bianco e nero

_____ 3. il poeta | c. gira un film western

_____ 4. la fotografa | d. dipinge una natura morta

_____ 5. la pittrice | e. compone una sinfonia

_____ 6. la regista | f. scolpisce una statua di marmo

_____ 7. lo scrittore | g. racconta una storia

_____ 8. lo scultore | h. scrive un romanzo giallo

8.4

In anagrams, the letters composing a word or a phrase can be rearranged to form another word or phrase: **amor** (*love*) → **roma** (*Rome*). The following words are anagrams of words found in Chapter 8. Take these anagrams and figure out the original words. At times an extra letter has been added, or taken out (in parentheses) to make the anagram possible.

1. allergia (-e) _____

2. alveare (+ f) _____

3. armi _____

4. creta _____

5. gela _____

6. mari _____

7. mozza _____

8. passaggio (-s; + e) _____

9. raspare _____

10. tira _____

11. tomo _____

12. tritato (+ r) _____

13. tuonare _____

14. visitare (-e) _____

8.5

You are the editor of an important newspaper. Match the following sections of the paper with the headlines that follow.

Le rubriche del giornale:

_____ 1. Editoriali

_____ 2. Esteri

_____ 3. Interni

_____ 4. Cronaca e Società

_____ 5. Economia e Finanza

_____ 6. Cultura

_____ 7. Spettacoli

_____ 8. Scienza e Tecnologia

_____ 9. Sport

Le notizie:

a. IL COMMENTO I giovani vogliono ancora il posto di lavoro fisso

b. DOSSIER ONU Il cemento divora le coste del Mediterraneo

c. BEBÈ E SOCIETÀ ITALIANA Il tasso italiano delle nascite è in leggero aumento

d. È ORA DI FARE LA DICHIARAZIONE DEI REDDITI

e. FINANZA E PENSIONI INTEGRATIVE Il crac della maggiore società di assicurazione europea mette in pericolo migliaia di pensioni

f. I NOSTRI ANTENATI, GLI ETRUSCHI I riti funerari degli etruschi e dei romani: una ricerca tra antropologia e mito

g. IL NOBEL PER LA PACE Il comitato svedese ha assegnato a El-Baredei il premio Nobel per la pace

h. IL NUOVO FILM DI MEL GIBSON

i. L'ECONOMIA DELL'UNIONE EUROPEA La BCE alza il tasso di sconto

j. LA GUERRA IN IRAQ Attentato a Baghdad: cinquanta civili iracheni e due soldati americani uccisi in un attentato

k. LA NANOTECNOLOGIA E L'UOMO ROBOTICO

l. LAICI E CATTOLICI Il Papa interviene nelle elezioni politiche italiane

m. LE LINGUE DEL MONDO Le lingue si estinguono come gli animali

n. OLIMPIADI INVERNALI: GRANDE VITTORIA PER L'ITALIA Alle Olimpiadi della neve, gli Azzurri vincono la medgalia d'oro nella staffetta di fondo

o. OMICIDIO RITUALE E MESSE NERE Calabria, dubbi sulla pista satanica nell'omicidio rituale di due fratelli

p. PRECARIATO E GLOBALIZZAZIONE Gli studenti scendono in piazza contro la nuova legge sul lavoro

q. SIAMO TUTTI DON CHISCHIOTTE? Mulini a vento ed energia rinnovabile

8.6

In the following sentences about sports and games, players and their equipment or activity are mismatched. Rearrange the words in each sentence so that each player can engage in his/her sport or game.

1. Il calciatore ha infilato la palla nel canestro.

   _____

2. Il calciatore ha vinto la gara alle parallele.

   _____

3. Il corridore ha rotto i bastoncini.

   _____

4. Il giocatore di basket ha messo la palla in porta.

   _____

5. La cavallerizza si è dimenticata la racchetta.

   _____

6. La ginnasta cercherà di bettere il record dei cento metri.

   _____

7. La golfista ha tirato il calcio di rigore.

   _____

8. La nostra squadra di baseball ha vinto il torneo regionale di pallavolo.

   _____

9. La squadra di pallavolo della scuola ha gettato l'ancora.

   _____

10. La tennista ha perso il torneo di baseball.

    _____

11. La velista è andata a cavallo nel bosco.

    _____

12. Lo sciatore di fondo ha mandato la pallina da golf nel lago.

    _____

9.1

You participated in a raffle and won a one-week hotel stay at the prestigious Hotel Danieli in Venice. Choose the correct words to complete each of the following sentences.

1. L'Hotel Danieli è un albergo a _____ .

a. due stelle   b. cinque stelle   c. tre soli

2. Il Danieli è situato _____ Piazza San Marco.

a. lontano da   b. vicino a   c. nel mezzo di

3. I prezzi variano dai 215 euro di una _____ , ai 2.648 euro per una suite _____ laguna.

a. camera singola; con vista sulla   b. suite, senza vista sulla   c. camera matrimoniale; lontana dalla

4. Vorrei _____ due _____ una per me e mia moglie e un bambino piccolo, e una per i miei due ragazzi.

a. disdire, posti   b. prenotare, posti   c. prenotare, camere

5. Ho bisogno di camere con l'aria _____ .

a. riscaldata   b. ventilata   c. condizionata

6. E per che _____ vuole prenotare?

a. periodo   b. secolo   c. piano

7. Ho bisogno del numero di una _____ per confermare la prenotazione.

a. assegno   b. biglietto aereo   c. carta di credito

9.2

Complete or answer the following sentences regarding traffic rules, choosing from among the options given below.

1. Il segnale 'vicolo cieco' vuol dire che _____ .

a. la strada è senza uscita
b. non si passa perché ci sono dei lavori in corso
c. la strada è troppo stretta per le automobili

2. Il segnale 'diritto di precedenza' vuol dire che _____ .

a. al prossimo incrocio devi rallentare o fermarti per lasciar passare chi arriva dall'altra strada
b. tutti devono fermarsi all'incrocio
c. chi ha il diritto di precedenza può andare avanti senza rallentare o fermarsi

3. Quando fai marcia indietro vuol dire che _____ .

a. hai cambiato idea riguardo alla tua destinazione
b. giri la macchina e vai nel senso opposto
c. cambi marcia e fai retrocedere la macchina senza girarla

4. Sei al volante, quando il tuo compagno di viaggio grida improvvisamente: "Sta' attento al pedone!" Che cosa sta succedendo?

_____

a. una persona a piedi vuole attrarre la tua attenzione
b. stai per investire una persona a piedi
c. una persona a piedi cerca di sorpassarti

5. A chi ti rivolgi se dici: "Mi faccia il pieno"? _____

a. il benzinaio
b. il vigile
c. il meccanico

6. Che cosa vuol dire 'fare il pieno'? _____

a. cambiare l'olio
b. riempire il serbatoio di benzina
c. essere veramente stufo della situazione

7. Su che mezzo di trasporto sei se il guidatore ti dice: "La corsa fino alla stazione le costerà circa 10 euro"? _____

a. un autobus
b. un treno
c. un taxi

8. Che cosa devi fare se vedi il cartello: 'Obbligo dei fari in galleria'?

_____

a. devi essere sicuro che i fari della tua automobile funzionino
b. devi accendere i fari prima di entrare in galleria
c. devi spegnere i fari prima di entrare in galleria

9. Il segnale 'lavori in corso' vuol dire che _____ .

a. stanno facendo delle riparazioni alla strada
b. ci sono dei lavori in uno dei corsi della città
c. c'è una deviazione al traffico

10. Ti hanno dato la multa per eccesso di velocità. Vuol dire che

_____ .

a. stavi andando troppo forte
b. stavi andando troppo piano
c. eri fermo

9.3

Choosing from among the following items, decide what activities you will do in each location. Collect the appropriate equipment and the number of items people will need. The same equipment may be necessary for different kinds of vacations.

arrampicare   arrivare in cima   camminare   costruire i castelli di sabbia

fare sub   i giocattoli per la spiaggia   i pasti liofilizzati   il termos

il materassino gonfiabile   il sacco   il sacco a pelo   il costume da bagno

l'antizanzare   l'ombrellone   la borraccia   la corda

la crema antisolare   la guida alpina   la mappa   la muta

la picozza   la pila   la sedia a sdraio   la tenda

le pinne   nuotare   prendere la tinaterella

1. Una settimana in un paesino sul mare. A te piace fare il sub, a tua moglie piace abbronzarsi e i tuoi due bambini giocano in spiaggia.

Equipaggiamento: _____

Attività: _____

2. Una settimana di alpinismo con la guida.

Equipaggiamento: _____

Attività: _____

3. Una settimana in un parco naturale (in tenda) con il tuo migliore amico o la tua migliore amica.

Equipaggiamento: _____

Attività: _____

10.1

Match the appropriate qualifier on the right to the noun on the left.

_____ 1. il diritto   a. alla privacy

_____ 2. i gruppi   b. antifascista

_____ 3. la classe   c. antiglobalizzazione

_____ 4. la discriminazione   d. comunisti

_____ 5. le dimostrazioni   e. etnica

_____ 6. la minoranza f. femminista

_____ 7. la resistenza g. media

_____ 8. la rivoluzione h. pacifisti

_____ 9. l'opinione i. per i diritti degli omosessuali

_____ 10. i regimi j. pubblica

_____ 11. il movimento k. razziale

10.2

Write the words corresponding to the following definitions. After you figure out each of these words, string them together and they will reveal a top secret message.

1. Segreto, da non rendere di pubblico dominio. _____
   (_masculine singular adjective_)

2. Qualsiasi complesso organico di forma militare. _____
   (_feminine plural noun_)

3. Chi è unito ad altri da un'alleanza. _____ (_feminine plural adjective_)

4. Scendere a terra da una nave. _____ (_intransitive verb, simple future, third-person plural_)

5. Attaccata a un sostantivo, stabilisce delle relazioni di luogo. _____ (_preposition_)

6. Regione della Francia nord occidentale. _____ (_name_)

7. Nega o esclude il concetto espresso dal verbo. _____ (_adverb_)

8. Attaccata a un sostantivo, stabilisce delle relazioni di luogo. _____ (_preposition_)

9. Cittadina della Francia nord orientale. _____ (_name_)

10. _____ (_feminine singular definite article_)

11. Tempo durante il quale una località non è illuminata dal sole. _____ (_feminine noun_)

12. Attaccata a un sostantivo, stabilisce una relazione di specificazione. _____ (_definite masculine singular article + preposition_)

13. Numero cardinale successivo di cinque. _____
    (*cardinal number*)

14. Sesto mese dell'anno nel calendario gregoriano. _____
    (*masculine noun*)

15. Numero che segue 1943. _____ (*cardinal number*)

10.3

Match the beginnings of the words on the left with the endings on the right.

1. buro _____	care
2. costitu _____	crazia
3. diver _____	co
4. do _____	gresso
5. giudi _____	rio
6. lai _____	tuta
7. mino _____	la
8. pro _____	ranza
9. prosti _____	sità
10. raz _____	zione
11. rego _____	vere
12. volonta _____	za

10.4

Decide whether the following statements are True or False.

_____ 1. I ladri possono arrestare i poliziotti.

_____ 2. In Italia non c'è la pena di morte.

_____ 3. La difesa rappresenta il popolo italiano in tribunale.

_____ 4. Il traffico di donne e bambini è un grave problema
internazionale.

_____ 5. In Spagna gli omosessuali possono sposarsi.

_____ 6. Il furto di identità è stato reso molto più facile dall'Internet.

_____ 7. L'evasione non è un reato.

_____ 8. Non c'è bisogno del giuramento quando si testimonia in tribunale.

_____ 9. Le donne non possono fare l'avvocato.

_____ 10. La tolleranza è un valore centrale della democrazia.

10.5

Match the following words with the categories shown below.

ambasciatore   arrendersi   attaccare   battaglia

bombardamento   carestia   consolato   cooperazione internazionale

dialogo   diritti umani   disarmo   disobbedienza civile

donazioni   evacuazione   genocidio   guerriglia

intervento umanitario   mediatore   non violenza   olocausto

pacifismo   puliza etnica   soccorso

solidarietà   terrorismo   tortura

1. forme di aggressione e combattimento: _____

2. pace e azioni di protesta: _____

3. questioni umanitarie: _____

11.1

Pair the partial sentences on the left with their appropriate conclusions on the right.

_____ 1. Alcune costellazioni   a. causate dalla Luna.

_____ 2. Di recente si è scoperto   b. con gli anelli.

_____ 3. Il pianeta più grande del   c. è compreso il sistema solare.

_____ 4. La Terra   d. danno il nome ai segni dello Zodiaco.

_____ 5. Le maree sono   e. le comete annunciassero disastri.

_____ 6. Le stelle cadenti   f. non ne esci più.

_____ 7. Nella Via Lattea   g. gira intorno al Sole.

_____ 8. Saturno è il pianeta

h. rappresentano l'amore e la guerra.

_____ 9. Se cadi in un buco nero

i. sistema solare è Giove.

_____10. Una volta si credeva che

j. sono numerose in estate.

_____11. Venere e Marte

k. un decimo pianeta.

11.2

Complete the following sentences choosing from among the words listed below each sentence.

1. I pianeti orbitano intorno al Sole grazie alla _____ .

a. gravità   b. rotazione   c. Via Lattea

2. La Terra è divisa in emisfero settentrionale e meridionale

   _____ .

a. dal Tropico del Cancro   b. dall'equatore   c. dai paralleli

3. Il cielo è blu perché la Terra ha _____ .

a. la stratosfera   b. l'aria   c. l'atmosfera

4. L'Italia è _____ .

a. una penisola   b. un'isola   c. un continente

5. I fiumi _____ nel mare.

a. si fermano   b. sfociano   c. scorrono

6. I ghiacciai si stanno _____ .

a. gelando   b. aprendo   c. sciogliendo

7. _____ di giugno corrisponde al giorno più lungo

   dell'anno.

a. Il solstizio   b. L'equinozio   c. La metà

11.3

You're taking a week-long vacation in New York in December. Are the following statements likely to be Correct or Incorrect?

1. La temperatura in questa stagione oscilla tra i 5 gradi (centigradi) sotto zero e i 10 sopra zero. _____

2. Le previsioni per la settimana tra il 15 e il 22 dicembre indicano sole caldo per i primi due giorni fino alle ore 19. _____

3. Per i giorni seguenti si prevedono temporali con grandine e piogge torrenziali. _____

4. Il sole sorgerà alle 5:45. _____

5. Per il 17, 18 e 19 dicembre si prevede cielo coperto con una temperatura massima di 12 gradi (centigradi). _____

6. Per il 20 dicembre si prevede una nevicata con temperatura minima di − 4 gradi (centigradi). _____

7. L'abbigliamento più adatto comprende un impermeabile ed una giacca pesante. _____

8. Si rischia il congelamento se si sta fermi in strada per più di dieci minuti. _____

11.4

Complete the following sentences, choosing from among the words listed below. More than one word may be appropriate.

fumi nocivi   anidride carbonica   particelle   decibel

disboscamento   la biomassa   il sole   il vento

riciclare   rinnovabili

1. L'inquinamento può essere da _____ .

2. L'inquinamento da rumore si misura in _____ .

3. L'effetto serra è casusato dall'accumulo di _____ nell'atmosfera.

4. Le fonti rinnovabili di energia includono _____ .

5. Per conservare energia dovremmo _____ tutti i rifiuti e usare solo fonti _____ .

6. Il _____ è una delle cause maggiori delle frane.

11.5

Place each of the following plants and animals in the appropriate climate zone and geographical environment.

il cammello   il cervo   il coccodrillo   il coyote   il falco

il fenicottero   il giaguaro   il lupo   il panda   il pappagallo

il passero   il pinguino   il rinoceronte   il serpente a sonagli   l'airone l'anatra   l'aquila   l'elefante   l'ippopotamo   l'orso

la foca   la gazzella   la giraffa   la leonessa   la scimmia

la tigre   la volpe   la zebra   lo scorpione

1. La savana _____

2. La zona polare _____

3. La zona temperata _____

4. La zona tropicale e la foresta equatoriale _____

5. Il deserto _____

12.1

Spell out the following arithmetical operations.

Example: $2 + 2 = 4 \rightarrow$ *Due più due fa quattro*

1. $10 - 5 = 5$ _____

2. $45 \div 5 = 9$ _____

3. $38 + 17 + 4 = 59$ _____

4. $54 \div 3 = 18$ _____

5. $18 \times 12 = 216$ _____

6. $495 - 231 = 264$ _____

7. $13,2 \times 16,5 = 217,8$ _____

8. $15 \times 3 \times 10 = 450$ _____

12.2

Write the words corresponding to the following definitions.

Circular shapes

1. Luogo dei punti del piano equidistanti da un punto fisso.
   _____ (*feminine noun*)

2. Distanza d'un punto qualsiasi della circonferenza dal centro.
   _____ (*masculine noun*)

3. Superficie piana racchiusa da una circonferenza. _____
   (*masculine noun*)

Polygonal shapes

4. Poligono con tre vertici. _____ (*masculine noun*)

5. Segmento o retta che limita una figura geometrica piana.
   _____ (*masculine noun*)

6. Porzione di piano compresa fra due semirette uscenti dallo stesso
   punto. _____ (*masculine noun*)

Quadrangles

7. Quadrangolo regolare, con i lati e gli angoli uguali.
   _____ (*masculine noun*)

8. Quadrilatero con tutti gli angoli retti. _____ (*masculine
   noun*)

9. In un poligono semplice, la retta che unisce due vertici non
   consecutivi. _____ (*feminine noun*)

10. Somma delle lunghezze dei lati di un poligono. _____
    (*masculine noun*)

11. Misura dell'estensione di una superficie. _____
    (*feminine noun*)

12.3

Add the appropriate adverb of time to the following sentences.

1. _____ tutti andavano a piedi.

2. _____ che lo vedo, mi ricorda che gli devo sei soldi.

3. Che noia! Parla _____ lui!

4. Il treno dei pendolari non è mai _____ .

5. La vedo _____ .

6. Non gli hai _____ parlato di quell'affare? Guarda che
   non abbiamo più molto tempo.

7. Non viene _____ a trovarmi.

8. Prima viene il Natale, _____ viene Santo Stefano.

9. Sei arrivata appena _____ per l'inizio del concerto.

10. Te l'ho detto _____ , _____ ,
    _____ di non giocare col computer fino a tardi.

12.4

Paying attention to the tense of the verb, add the appropriate adverb of time to the following sentences.

al giovedì mattina   di giorno   di notte   di venerdì

nei prossimi   passata   venerdì

1. Abbiamo deciso di partire il prossimo _____ .

2. Giochiamo a tennis sempre _____ .

3. Si ritiene che la temperatura del pianeta continuerà ad aumentare
   _____ decenni.

4. Lavora _____ e dorme _____ !

5. La settimana _____ faceva un freddo infernale.

6. Vai sempre al cinema _____ ?

Answer Key

1.1

1. la nascita	2. il telefono	3. il signore / le signore
4. le scuse	5. la domanda	6. il fax / i fax
7. l(a)'operatrice	8. il / la centralinista	9. le pagine gialle
10. il / la / i / le single	11. il direttore	12. il regalo
13. il Capodanno	14. i nomi	15. il cognome
16. l(a)'occupazione	17. i luoghi	18. la / le gaffe
19. i cellulari	20. l(o)'interno.	

1.2

1. c　　　2. a　　　3. c　　　4. b

1.3

1. gentile	2. addio	3. arrivederci
4. grazie	5. domanda	6. comportamento
7. prego	8. scusa	9. permesso
10. favore		

1.4

1. c　　　2. g　　　3. e　　　4. d　　　5. f
6. b　　　7. a

1.5

1. un numero verde	2. l'interno	3. pronto
4. il telefonino	5. il cordless	6. messaggi
7. parlare	8. il centralino	

1.6

1. regalare	2. vi scuserete	3. telefonano
4. manderò due righe	5. chiedere	6. saluta
7. ringraziare		

1.7

1. quando	2. perché	3. che cosa
4. perché	5. come	6. dove
7. quanto	8. quanti	9. che cosa
10. chi	11. chi	12. chi

1.8

1. a	2. con	3. per	4. per
5. sul	6. in	7. dalla	8. da
9. tra	10. di		

1.9

1. c	2. b	3. a	4. a
5. c	6. c	7. b	8. a
9. c			

2.1

1. Yes	2. Yes	3. No	4. Yes
5. No	6. Yes	7. No	

2.2

1. assomiglia	2. preoccuparti	3. piace; piace
4. sanno	5. conoscono	6. pensa
7. cavarmela	8. capite	

2.3

1. voglio	2. Sa	3. devono
4. lasciate	5. sanno/possono	

2.4

1. zio	2. nipoti	3. cognato
4. suocera	5. suoceri	6. figlio
7. nipote	8. sorella	9. parenti
10. amante	11. zia	12. figli

2.5

1. brutto	2. piccolo	3. buono	4. forte
5. allegro	6. stupido		

2.6

1. essere	2. avere	3. avere	4. avere	5. avere
6. avere	7. avere	8. essere	9. avere	10. avere
11. essere	12. essere	13. essere	14. avere	15. avere
16. avere	17. avere	18. avere	19. essere	20. avere
21. essere	22. essere	23. avere	24. essere	

3.1

1. le braccia
2. le gambe
3. lo stomaco
4. le ginocchia
5. la bocca
6. il cervello
7. le mani
8. la mano
9. le orecchie
10. gli occhi

3.2

1. camminare
2. masticare
3. guardare; toccare
4. sentire
5. baciare
6. ascoltare
7. assaggiare
8. digerire
9. indicare
10. vedere

3.3

1. No
2. Yes
3. No
4. No
5. Yes
6. No

3.4

1. l'ospedale
2. help
3. thank you
4. prego
5. infarto
6. esami
7. esame

3.5

1. magro
2. bene
3. male
4. adolescenza
5. mano
6. bocca
7. donna
8. cura
9. testa
10. dieta
11. vita
12. vena
13. rene
14. sano
15. diabete
16. dentista
17. morire
18. guarire

3.6

1. f
2. e
3. a
4. b
5. g
6. i
7. h
8. d
9. c

3.7

1. nascere, crescere, invecchiare, morire

2. dare alla luce, allattare, tirare su, seppellire

3. giovane, adulto, di mezza età, anziano

4. infanzia, pubertà, adolescenza, vecchiaia

4.1

1. a	2. c	3. b	4. b	5. c
6. a	7. a	8. b	9. b	10. c

4.2

1. to crash	2. to click	3. to backup
4. click	5. diskette	6. laptop
7. cybernetics	8. interface	9. memory
10. battery	11. display	12. to reboot

4.3

1. disciplines: agraria, l'amministrazione aziendale, l'educazione civica, la biologia, la geometria, la giurisprudenza, la medicina, la psicologia

2. degrees and certifications: l'abilitazione, l'esame di ammissione, l'esame di stato, la laurea

3. professions and roles in the field of education and research: il rettore, il ricercatore, l'insegnante, la bibliotecaria, la maestra

4. activities and institutions: il corso, il dipartimento, il politecnico, il conservatorio, il seminario, il voto, l'esame, la biblioteca, la pagella, le tasse universitarie

5. actions: copiare, dare il voto, discutere la tesi, fare l'appello, fare lezione, insegnare, iscriversi all'università, laurearsi, ritirarsi da un corso, tagliare

4.4

1. b	2. c	3. a	4. c	5. d

5.1

1. b	2. c	3. c	4. a	5. c

5.2

a. a week-long business trip in March: 2, 6, 8, 9, 10, 11, 13, 15, 17, 19

b. a weekend in the countryside in November: 1, 2, 3, 7, 9, 10, 14, 18, 19

c. a relaxing, though slightly cold winter afternoon at home: 1, 3, 7, 9, 14, 18, 24

d. opening night at the Opera in October: 4, 5, 16, 23

e. a dinner out with friends in a trendy restaurant: 12, 20, 21, 22

5.3

1. A man's fashion show.
2. Fall-winter 2006.
3. For a young man.
4. Informal.
5. It is a striped jacket.
6. They are sporty.
7. Alaska.
8. A tent.
9. Down.
10. It is water-repellent.
11. Brave the lowest temperatures without any problem.
12. The most famous universities in the world where entomology is studied.
13. Cotton or jersey.
14. Sweaters, sweatshirts, and bags.
15. The university's address and logo are printed on it.

5.4

1. Sono in farmacia.
2. Sono andati in latteria.
3. Entriamo dal fruttivendolo.
4. Passano tutti i pomeriggi in gelateria.
5. Sono passata per caso dal gioielliere.
6. In salumeria c'era troppa gente.
7. Hai chiesto in drogheria?

6.1

1. un grattacielo
2. l'aria condizionata
3. senza ascensore
4. in una cascina
5. una cooperativa
6. in centro
7. Attenti al cane!
8. le chiavi
9. in soffitta
10. in cortile
11. una casa prefabbricata

6.2

Inserzione: Cercasi casa unifamigliare a Roma, in quartiere semi-centrale, parco e scuole medie superiori vicine, con doppio garage, giardino, cucina abitabile, quattro camere da letto, tre bagni, tasso fisso, trenta per cento di caparra.

6.3

1. a   2. c   3. b

6.4

1. c   2. b   3. b   4. a   5. c

6.5

1. spegnere
2. svegliarsi
3. coricarsi
4. aprire
5. vendere
6. scongelare
7. salire le scale
8. apparecchiare
9. pulire
10. entrare

6.6

First Courses

Spaghetti carbonara
with sautéed pancetta, garlic, olive oil, dry white wine, eggs, parmesan cheese, and chopped parsley

Grandmother-style butterfly pasta
with red onion, rosemary, gorgonzola, and walnut cream sauce

Egg fettuccine Genovese-style
with basil pesto with sautéed shrimp, roasted peppers, and peeled tomatoes

Risotto with seafood
with shrimp sautéed in olive oil and garlic

Three-cheese gnocchi
potato gnocchi with fontina, gorgonzola, parmigiano, and a butter and sage sauce

Desserts

Tiramisu
Ladyfingers dipped in rum and coffee and covered with a cream sauce made with eggs, cocoa, and sugar

Wild berries
raspberries, strawberries, and blueberries in dry sparkling white wine and sugar

Fruit salad
grapes, bananas, peaches, apricots, kiwis, and pineapple in a lemon/lime and sugar juice

7.1

1. pubblico impiego; finanza; credito/assicurazioni

2. editoria, telecomunicazioni, spettacolo, lingue, pubblicità

7.2

1. attività commerciali	2. editoria, pubblicità	3. informatica
4. turismo	5. attività commerciali	6. attività commerciali, altre attività
7. attività commerciali	8. attività commerciali	9. sanità
10. sanità	11. amministrazione	12. agricoltura
13. ambiente/ecologia	14. industria	15. informatica
16. finanza	17. Internet	18. finanza
19. amministrazione	20. altre attività	21. editoria
22. Internet	23. ambiente/ecologia	24. sanità

7.3

1. no	2. no	3. eight
4. private	5. the ones that give stock options to their managers	6. private

7.4

1. logo	2. tradizione	3. Fabbrica
4. azionista	5. Direttore	6. Europa
7. pista	8. automobili	9. veicoli
10. boom	11. mercato	12. estero
13. sindacato	14. scioperi	15. economici
16. lavoratori	17. stabilimenti	18. produzione
19. personale	20. accordo	21. modelli
22. design	23. tecnico	

7.5

1. il bilancio	2. il brevetto	3. il cambio
4. la concorrenza	5. il costo	6. la domanda
7. l'economia	8. economico	9. l'efficienza
10. la finanza	11. gestire	12. l'inflazione
13. il monopolio	14. la multinazionale	15. l'offerta
16. la produttività	17. la ripresa	18. la valuta

8.1

1. il domatore
2. il pianista
3. la conduttrice [televisiva]
4. la ballerina
5. il giocoliere
6. il direttore d'orchestra
7. l'attrice [di cinema]
8. lo spettatore
9. il radiocronista
10. gli acrobati
11. il clown
12. il disc jockey
13. la modella
14. l'architetto
15. il vasaio
16. la funambola

8.2

1. False
2. True
3. False
4. False
5. False
6. True
7. True
8. False

8.3

1. e.
2. g.
3. a.
4. b.
5. d.
6. c.
7. h.
8. f.

8.4

1. argilla
2. fare vela
3. mira
4. carte
5. lega
6. rima
7. mazzo
8. paesaggio
9. sparare
10. arti
11. moto
12. ritratto
13. nuotare
14. rivista

8.5

1. a.
2. g., j.
3. l., p.
4. b., c., o.
5. d., e., i.
6. f., m.
7. h.
8. k., q.
9. n.

8.6

1. Il calciatore ha messo la palla in porta.
2. Il calciatore ha tirato il calcio di rigore.
3. Il corridore cercherà di bettere il record dei cento metri.
4. Il giocatore di basket ha infilato la palla nel canestro.
5. La cavallerizza è andata a cavallo nel bosco.
6. La ginnasta ha vinto la gara alle parallele.
7. La golfista ha mandato la pallina da golf nel lago.
8. La nostra squadra di baseball ha perso il torneo di baseball.
9. La squadra di pallavolo della scuola ha vinto il torneo regionale di pallavolo.
10. La tennista si è dimenticata la racchetta.

11. La velista ha gettato l'ancora.
12. Lo sciatore di fondo ha rotto i bastoncini.

9.1

1. b	2. b	3. a	4. c	5. c
6. a	7. c			

9.2

1. a	2. c	3. c	4. b	5. a
6. b	7. c	8. b	9. a	10. a

9.3

1. Equipaggiamento: quattro costumi da bagno; quattro sedie a sdraio; i giocattoli per la spiaggia; la crema antisolare; un materassino gonfiabile; un ombrellone; un paio di pinne; una muta. Attività: costruire i castelli di sabbia; fare sub; nuotare; prendere la tintarella.

2. Equipaggiamento: un sacco; un sacco a pelo; una borraccia; una guida alpina; una mappa; una picozza; della corda. Attività: arrampicare; arrivare in cima.

3. Equipaggiamento: due sacchi a pelo; due borracce; i pasti liofilizzati; l'antizanzare; un termos; una mappa; una pila; una tenda. Attività: camminare.

10.1

1. a	2. h	3. g	4. k	5. c
6. e	7. b	8. f	9. j	10. d
11. i				

10.2

Riservato. Le truppe alleate sbarcheranno in Normandia, non a Calais, la notte del sei giugno 1944.

10.3

1. burocrazia	2. costituzione	3. diversità
4. dovere	5. giudicare	6. laico
7. minoranza	8. progresso	9. prostituta
10. razza	11. regola	12. volontario

10.4

1. False   2. True   3. False   4. True   5. True
6. True   7. False   8. False   9. False   10. True

10.5

1. forme di aggressione e combattimento: arrendersi, attaccare, battaglia, bombardamento, genocidio, guerriglia, olocausto, puliza etnica, terrorismo, tortura

2. pace e azioni di protesta: ambasciatore, consolato, dialogo, disarmo, disobbedienza civile, mediatore, non violenza, pacifismo

3. questioni umanitarie: carestia, cooperazione internazionale, diritti umani, donazioni, evacuazione, intervento umanitario, soccorso, solidarietà

11.1

1. d   2. k   3. i   4. g   5. a
6. j   7. c   8. b   9. f   10. e
11. h

11.2

1. a   2. b   3. c   4. a   5. b
6. c   7. a

11.3

1. Correct   2. Incorrect   3. Incorrect   4. Incorrect   5. Correct
6. Correct   7. Correct   8. Incorrect

11.4

1. da anidride carbonica, da particelle, da fumi nocivi
2. decibel
3. di anidride carbonica
4. il sole, il vento, la biomassa
5. riciclare; rinnovabili
6. disboscamento

11.5

1. La savana: il giaguaro, il rinoceronte, l'elefante, l'ippopotamo, la gazzella, la giraffa, la leonessa, la zebra

2. La zona polare: il pinguino, la foca, l'orso

3. La zona temperata: il cervo, il coyote, il falco, il lupo, il panda, il passero, l'airone, l'anatra, l'aquila, l'orso, la volpe

4. La zona tropicale e la foresta equatoriale: il coccodrillo, il fenicottero, il pappagallo, la scimmia

5. Il deserto: il serpente a sonagli, lo scorpione, il cammello

12.1

1. Dieci meno cinque fa cinque
2. Quarantacinque diviso cinque fa nove
3. Trentotto più diciassette più quattro fa cinquantanove
4. Cinquantaquattro diviso tre fa diciotto
5. Diciotto moltiplicato dodici fa duecentosedici
6. Quattrocentonovantacinque meno duecentotrentuno fa duecentosessantaquattro
7. Tredici virgola due moltiplicato sedici virgola cinque fa duecentodiciassette virgola otto
8. Quindici moltiplicato tre moltiplicato dieci fa quattrocentocinquanta

12.2

1. la circonferenza	2. il raggio	3. il cerchio
4. il triangolo	5. il lato	6. l'angolo
7. il quadrato	8. il rettangolo	9. la diagonale
10. il perimetro	11. l'area	

12.3

1. Una volta	2. Ogni volta	3. sempre
4. in orario	5. di rado	6. ancora
7. mai	8. dopo	9. in tempo
10. una volta, due volte, tre volte		

12.4

1. venerdì	2. al giovedì mattina	3. nei prossimi
4. di notte; di giorno	5. passata	6. di venerdì